Praise 1
Mexico, A Lo

"Twenty-two distinctive and uniq_ through an exhausting and passionate range of emotions. The book is alive with love and laughter, tears and tenderness, death—and voices from the spirit world. Reading it is like inhaling a culture in all its dimensions. Like the richness of Mexico, the book sizzles with the heat and heart of the Mexican people and pulses through women in love."

—Rita Golden Gelman, author of *Tales of a Female Nomad*

"This insightful collection of stories is filled with vivid descriptions and engaging characters. Women write about their love affair with Mexico and reveal a complicated lover imbued with beauty, passion, danger, and excitement that will lead them to a transformative experience."

—Rose Castillo Guilbault, author of *Farmworker's Daughter: Growing Up Mexican In America*

"Nearly two dozen American women wander into the vast world-next-door that is our neighbor to the south. With equal measures of curiosity and courage, they journey to sunny resorts, grim penitentiaries, and time-challenged villages. Like them, you will be enchanted and amazed."

—Héctor Tobar, author of *Translation Nation: Defining a New American Identity in the Spanish-Speaking United States*

"With open minds and hearts, these writers engage Mexico in all its sensual, spiritual, confounding glory and emerge transformed."
—Gina Hyams, author of *In a Mexican Garden*

"This wide-ranging collection of gringa experiences in Mexico shines a light upon, and becomes a part of, one of the most charged cultural conversations on earth: that between North Americans and their southern neighbors."
—Tony Cohan, author of *On Mexican Time* and *Mexican Days*

"In this book, a love of Mexico flows from many springs. An L.A. teenager goes 'home' to Oaxaca once a year. A woman goes on vacation and stays seventeen years. Some fall in love with colors, food, the sea; some discover themselves in their interactions with the people they meet. What is common to all their stories is an openness to experience, an eagerness to transcend the familiar self. Sometimes there's hurt, too, because real travel, like real life, is not covered with a warranty. These wonderful myriad voices remind us that getting away is sometimes the real route home."
—Sandra Scofield, author of *Gringa* and *Occasions of Sin: A Memoir*

Praise for
France, A Love Story

"This is a very readable collection. . . . Tales are alternately loving, witty, nostalgic, and, yes, occasionally swooning."
—*San Francisco Chronicle*

"The heart of this book is in the maturity of its voices of experience."
—*Boston Globe*

"In this beautiful collection, women share their experiences first-hand, reflecting on the ways France's unique culture has enriched and enchanted their lives."
—*France Today*

"This book is an evocative gathering of short pieces from twenty-five female writers. . . . This is a collection that will be appreciated by the Francophiles among us."
—*Toronto Globe and Mail*

Greece,

A Love Story

Edited by
Camille Cusumano

SEAL PRESS

Greece, A Love Story
Women Write about the Greek Experience

"Yeia sas!" originally appeared as *"Yassas!"* in *Resident Abroad*. Copyright © 1987 by Susan M. Tiberghien.

 Published by
Seal Press
An Imprint of Avalon Publishing Group, Incorporated
1400 65th Street, Suite 250
Emeryville, CA 94608

ISBN-13: 978-1-58005-197-2
ISBN-10: 1-58005-197-9

A Note on Language
Please note that for consistency and clarity, we have simplified the use of accents on Greek words and transliterated the names of certain names and places to approximate spoken Greek.

Cover and interior design by Tabitha Lahr
Cover photo © Macduff Everton/Corbis
Printed in the United States of America
Distributed by Publishers Group West

Contents

Introduction

Greece, it has been said, was where art became inseparable from life. How often do we invoke the Platonic ideal or the Golden Age of Pericles as the highest standard by which to measure the merit of an idea, a work of art, a way of living? We do this because Greece has bequeathed civilization unparalleled gifts of beauty and wisdom, from its delicate pottery, gracefully sculpted statues, and the well-proportioned Parthenon and Acropolis to the enduring literature of Homer, Sappho, and Sophocles, not to mention Socratic discourse, Aristotelian thought, the first Olympic Games, our own democracy, and let's not forget moussaka, spanakopita, and souvlaki.

1

So it follows that each travel essay in this collection is a unique blend of artistry and life. For example, in Alison Cadbury's story we enter Greece by way of her fantasy writer's retreat, a quiet home in the Greek countryside. Ah, but there's a crack in this idyll, and he goes by the name of Kosmas. The ninety-year-old landlord drops by unbidden and shouts, "Wake up, lazy girl . . . and make me a coffee!" When you learn why he does this, you understand why she allows this natty Greek gent to continue this way.

This writer, along with the other authors in this anthology, offers the reader her Greek experience as a slice of life that transcends the typical surface treatment of the go-here, go-there travel article.

Katherina Audley takes the reader to that ubiquitous corner of Greece—the taverna. She relates her amazing tale almost entirely from atop a bar, where she dances nightly even as her inner anthropologist observes rituals such as smashing dishes or making *kamaki*, "the Greek man's prerogative to attempt courtship with every female who crosses his path." And there's Linda Hefferman, "a strange blond girl wearing pants," who carries all the way from her hometown mortician an envelope of American dollars and family memorabilia for this former Greek patriot's cousin. The ensuing task of eating the grateful Greek family's lovingly prepared goat entrails resonates as a metaphor for the difficulty of swallowing parts of a culture alien to our palate. Yet, Hefferman persists.

But Pamela S. Stamatiou is the paragon of such persistence. Her story about her romance and marriage to a Greek man is that bittersweet sort, offering up the intricacies of Greek ways and the pain and pleasure of assimilation in an old-world patriarchal culture that most of us will never experience.

Like Stamatiou, Colleen McGuire is an expat married to a Greek man—and, for better or worse, to her bicycle. It is purely delightful to travel with her by way of her two-wheeled steed to many of the Greek isles, including Lesvos, Pserimos, Kos (the Dodecanese homeland of Hippocrates), and Paros, where she climbs to the Valley of the Butterflies. Recalling how the Greeks raised athleticism to an art form, we want to cheer her on when she debates whether to accept the challenge of a day-long, 150–mile bike odyssey.

Given that Greece still holds many vestiges of its cult of the Great Mother, it seems fitting to include three moving stories that explore the mother-daughter bond. In Liza Monroy's coming-of-age piece, she visits her expat mother in Greece and makes her "journey into adulthood," sweetly recalling Greece as the country where the three Fates wove together "my past, present, and future."

The spirit of that famous mother-daughter duo, Demeter and Persephone, also imbues Diane LeBow's essay, in which she takes her fun-loving eighty-year-old mother to flirt and frolic on a Greek tour. Later she returns to cast her mother's ashes to the wind and sea. Simone Butler takes her mother's ashes, too, and mingles them with Greek soil. Her quest is for inner peace with her mother's untimely death, and she finds it in a small "mama church" en route to the cave of mighty Zeus. After her younger sister's death from cancer, Marilyn McFarlane, too, finds solace in visiting such places as Delphi's sacred way and the ancient *hospital* of Epidaurus.

Amanda Castleman's essay offers one of this collection's most brilliant examples of how art and life are inseparable. One morning in Athens, Castleman's husband serves her sweet morning Greek pastry along with the bitter news that he wants a divorce. In telling her story, Castleman writes prose that would make Henry Miller, acclaimed author of *The Colossus of Maroussi*, turn green with envy: "Plum shadows outline the Parthenon. This buttress of land, the art upon it—defying time and Turkish detonations—are so ancient. The moon even more so, a bruised apricot. My woes, suspended briefly between the two, have no weight."

If, as I do, you savor such well-honed prose, the kind that reveals a story equal to its labor, read Ashley Black. She goes to the mountains of northern Greece in search of the biological parents she only learned about after years of an uncanny passion for all things Greek. Again, it is the telling as much as the outcome of her search that draws us deep into a Greece we might never have known.

One has to be brave when reading Davi Walders's and Susan Tiberghien's stories. Walders writes how Rhodes, "officially the sunniest place in Europe," holds one of Greece's darkest chapters—that of the Rhodian Jews who did not survive the Nazi roundups and deportations. Walders's story unfolds through one of the few survivors, whom she serendipitously meets in Rhodes. Similarly, Tiberghien and her husband, just passing through a village in Crete, are taken in by an amiable Greek guide. Amid the pink flowers of a dittany-covered hillside, "the blossoming love bed of Zeus and Europa," they learn how their kind host lost his only child, a girl of fifteen, to the Germans during World War II. Even as Tiberghien now sees the flowered hills as "scarred battlefields," we realize that here is what we all long for when we travel—the depth and breadth of the whole story, the blinding, life-giving sun, as well as the darkening skies of past mistakes. We want to know that gardens grow over battlegrounds and that soft centers lie beneath leathery skin.

Once, a long time ago, I visited this isle-perforated land of scintillating whites and impossible blues. I slept on beaches and drank ouzo and retsina. I ate the unforgettable cream of yogurts and wrapped my tongue around a few Greek phrases. I thought I had been there, had experienced the culture—until I had the pleasure of working with these stories. Now I know better. With each story, I am carried back there; I am broadened. I hope every reader will be, too.

Camille Cusumano
March 2007

Sarah McCormic

Kostas and the Deep Sea

The ferry rocked and dipped through the dark, headed for a tiny island that my guidebook called "the Aegean's hidden treasure." In fact, so few tourists visited the island that it had no actual hotels, according to the book. I'd have to rent a room in someone's home. And since the place had few telephones, I couldn't even call ahead to book a room. The only boat there departed from a slightly larger island just a few times a week, at dawn. "You won't regret taking the extra trouble," my book promised. "This little island is a slice of old Greece."

As the sky lightened, the ferry's other passengers began to stir, stretching and shuffling to the windows to squint at the fog. I realized I was the only tourist and the only woman on the boat. The others were old men in dark suits and caps, or young men in T-shirts and jeans. I smiled at an old man whose face seemed kind, but he grimaced and dropped his head, studying his feet. A moment later, the fog parted and our ferry stopped. We filed down a narrow ramp onto an empty stone pier. There were no buildings or cars or people to greet us, just the sounds of waves slapping against stone and a cranky gull squawking from a nearby rock. I followed the others along a road that zigzagged up the side of a dark cliff.

When I reached the top, my lungs heaving, the men had disappeared. I found myself alone, leaning against a low stone wall, looking at the kind of view that is so unexpected and wondrous that your mind takes a picture and stores it forever. On the other side of the wall, the cliff plunged hundreds of feet, disappearing into the sea, a glittering expanse of pink and violet that stretched to the horizon. To the left, perched like a dare at the cliff's edge, a jumble of buildings huddled together, shaped like children's blocks and white as clean teeth. I felt dizzy from a mixture of joy and vertigo.

"*Dhomatio?*" A woman waved to me from across the road. She looked like someone from a fairytale: the archetypal old-world matron, stout, square, and hunched, as if everything vital had been drained out of her. A shapeless black dress hung down to her ankles. *"Dhomatio?"* she repeated, waving me to come closer. This Greek granny couldn't mean any harm, I figured. As I walked toward her, I saw that she was rather young—barely forty. *"Ella do, ella do"* (This way, this way), she said, pointing toward town.

I nodded and followed her home to a plain, white cube attached to the side of a larger building that I figured was her family's house. She handed me a key and left. My little room was as plain and white inside as it was outside, with a door that opened to a tiny alley, rough wooden shutters for windows, and a cross hanging over the bed. Eager to explore my "slice of old Greece," I left and crept shyly around the town, enchanted by the white stucco buildings with bright blue shutters, the pink oleander that climbed walls and spilled over rooftops, and the streets, snaking haphazardly between the buildings, paved in large, smooth stones and designed far too narrow for even the tiniest car. I walked from one end of town to the other in less than five minutes, meeting six filthy cats, a boy leading a donkey, and three ancient men in dark suits whose eyes fled mine. Everything was going according to plan: It was the perfect little Greek island, chock-full of tradition and old-world charm.

Three days later, I was having doubts. I sat alone at an outdoor taverna at the edge of town, where narrow alleys gave way to the island's rocky brown hills. It was midday in July, uncomfortably hot, and I was bored and lonely—and stranded. I had just been to the *plateia* (town square) to buy a ticket for the next ferry, but the man had shooed me away. *"Aperyia! Aperyia!"* he said. "Strike. Strike."

"How long?" I asked.

He rolled his eyes. "One week? Two weeks? Nobody can know."

I had already walked around the town's ancient streets, eaten steaming moussaka at a rickety wooden table in the quintessential *plateia*, ridden on the island's only bus down its only paved road to its heavenly beaches—crescents of white sand lapped by gentle turquoise waves. I was ready to tackle another island.

I ordered another soda and cursed the strike, wishing there were other tourists to talk to. I hadn't had a conversation in three days. Everywhere I went, I saw clusters of men and boys— hunched over backgammon boards in the *plateia*, sipping coffee in the tavernas. When they saw me coming, they ducked their heads and fell silent. As for the women, the only ones I saw were the old-world mamas in long black dresses who served me dinner. Giddy from the afternoon heat, I mused that the island's young women had been placed under a protective spell that rendered them invisible to outsiders' eyes. I sipped my soda and imagined them walking by unseen, giggling and pointing at my short, blond hair, picking up my napkin when I dropped it at dinner, riding beside me on the bus to the beach. I wished one of them would appear and talk to me.

Suddenly, the taverna came alive: Rowdy and laughing, yelling in Greek, a group of young people filled the remaining tables. *"Bires!"* they called to the waiter. Soon their tables were covered in beer bottles and plates of calamari. I noticed they were all boys, with one amazing girl. She wore a shiny black bikini top and cutoff jeans. Her nails were painted silver. Her eyes were lined in thick black eyeliner. Her jet black hair was cut in a blunt bob just below her ears, with bangs cut straight across her forehead—just like Cleopatra. She turned to me and raised an exquisite eyebrow. "Why don't you join us?" It was my first experience of Katerina's charms.

By the end of the day, half-drunk in the bar she owned with her boyfriend, Markos, Katerina put an arm around my waist and claimed me. "I saw from your face that you are a girl who likes fun. You must not leave me." She yelled something to Markos, who nodded from behind the bar and started making another of the strong, pink drinks that were making my head spin pleasantly. "For months, I am alone with only boys." She shook her head.

"Boys are very dull, you know," she said, placing a conspiratorial hand on my knee. "And of course, the local girls are not permitted to talk to me!"

Katerina told me she was from Thessaloniki, a city on the Greek mainland. She and Markos had fallen in love while working together at a bar on a neighboring island and decided to find another island and open their own bar. "I love this island the first moment I see it. It is beautiful. The beaches are perfect. The people are traditional, but they are good. It is the true Greece."

I looked around at Katerina's bar. As far as I could tell, it was the only bar on the island and bore little resemblance to what I thought of as "the true Greece." It was tiny—a single room I could cross in four long strides—but Katerina told me that they had modeled it after the big nightclubs in Athens: walls painted bright pink, lights tinted purple, a mirror behind a bar stocked with row upon row of expensive-looking liquors, and techno music played so loud it was like a second pulse. Markos tended bar. Katerina flitted between the bar and the sound system, where she donned headphones to queue up the next tape. She had changed into red leather pants and a silver halter top; a large gold cross hung between her breasts. In the far corner, a group of young men snickered into their beers, avoiding my gaze. "These local boys cannot speak English," Katerina said. "But they are sweet. I think they are a little afraid of you."

I told her about the boat strike. Her face lit up. "Wonderful! You can stay here and help me," she said. "I need another deejay."

After that, it was as if I had always been there. In the mornings, Katerina and I breakfasted in the shade of an olive tree in the *plateia*. She introduced me to the best yogurt I ever tasted, before or since. Made on the island by the old women, it was richer than homemade ice cream and had a slight sour tang that curled my lip. To offset the tang, we smothered it in honey. "It is the best yogurt in Greece," Katerina said. After breakfast, we went to the beach, where we exhausted ourselves swimming and sunbathing, then climbed a hill to an empty taverna that opened its kitchen just to serve us omelets, fried potatoes, and cold beer. In the afternoons, we parted to nap through the heat. At night, we met again at the bar, where Katerina appeared in another fantastic costume, glamorous as a movie star, regal as Cleopatra. She was the coolest person I had ever met. I found it ironic that I, the supposedly modern, savvy American, dressed so shabbily in my practical but plain wrinkle-free pants and T-shirts stained and misshapen from months of hand-washing in hotel bathroom sinks, while she looked ready for a fashion show runway. But she never seemed to notice the difference, instead treating me as if *I* were the glamorous one, as if she found *my* company irresistible.

I couldn't believe the life I was living. I barely recognized myself. On this little island, everything was light and fun—even me. It all felt too good to be true, and this began to worry me.

I turned my worry on Katerina. It seemed to me that she and Markos were living in a charming fantasy, having built a bar for a clientele that didn't exist. Each night, the customers were the same: their three friends visiting from Athens and the same four local boys. They must have been losing money. I rarely paid for my drinks, and Katerina was too generous to charge the local boys.

"This island is so quiet," I said. "Will there be more tourists later in the year?"

Katerina shrugged. "Maybe. Maybe not. Now, business is not so good, of course. But we think the tourists will come, and they will find our nice little bar, and they will like it! What is not to like? You tell me something you do not like, and I change it." She put down her drink and swept an arm, palm up, in front of her, presenting the room for my appraisal.

"I would change nothing," I said, meaning it. I loved this strange little bar where the music was too loud and I was the only customer. But Katerina's casual attitude made me anxious.

"How do you know that more tourists will come?" I asked. "What if . . ."

Katerina laid her hand on my cheek and shushed me. "Only God knows, right?" She clinked her glass against mine. "For the present, we live well!"

I looked away. "You know, I need to leave when the strike is over," I said. "The man at the ticket office said it may end in a few days." I would be sad to leave but was determined to stick to my travel plans, so I couldn't linger too long in paradise with Katerina.

"What is this 'keep on track'?" Katerina said. "Are you a train?" She grabbed my hand. "Come look at the stars with me, Sarah." We went out to the patio in front of the taverna, where we often sat, and shared a cigarette.

Katerina took a puff and squinted up at the stars. "If I get you a lover, then you will stay." Close by, in the darkness, a chicken clucked its disapproval. I giggled, thinking Katerina was joking. I should have known better.

"Him, I guess." I pointed to a boy with wavy hair the color of wet beach sand and an extra layer of boyish fat. He looked like a young Greek Bill Clinton, dribbling the ball calmly toward the basket, sweat sliding down his temples in the late afternoon heat. A crowd of scrawny, raven-haired boys cheered from the dusty perimeter of the makeshift outdoor court—a slab of concrete ringed by wooden benches borrowed from a nearby taverna.

My Greek Bill Clinton cut effortlessly around his opponent and sunk an impressive outside shot. The raven-haired boys went wild.

"That one? His name is Christos," Katerina said. "Okay. I take care of everything."

That night, Christos came to the bar for the first time. Later, he came back to my room.

"First, my first," he said, grinning. "Thank you."

I sat up in bed. Holy Zeus, he's a virgin. "How old are you?" Christos smiled up at me, brushing my shoulder with the back of his hand. "Seventeen."

I wasn't much older—barely twenty-one—but I was sure I had just broken some Greek law. *This is where it all goes wrong,* I thought. *This is where I pay for living so carelessly.* Then I thought of the Greek gods—disguising themselves as animals to trick their lovers, seducing other gods' wives, sleeping with sea nymphs. . . . This whole situation was so strange and dangerous and totally unlike me. And I kind of liked it. Christos looked me in the eyes and murmured something in Greek, over and over, like a song, until I lay back down and forgot to be afraid.

"I will stay a few more days," I told Katerina the next morning at breakfast. She licked the honey off her spoon and smiled, saying nothing.

From then on, I met Christos each night at the bar. I didn't fool myself that we were falling in love. He spoke so little English that our conversations were limited to a few words. I told myself he was with me because there was no one else; the local girls, locked up by their watchful parents, were completely off-limits.

Besides, falling in love in Greece, thousands of miles from home, wouldn't make sense.

"What do you do all day?" I asked him one night. I had never seen him at the beach or eating breakfast in the *plateia*.

"Make house," he said.

"Oh—construction? You build houses?"

He nodded, then kissed me until I had no more questions.

A few days later, I saw Christos at work. It was a sweltering midsummer day. I was on my way home for a nap after a day at the beach. Christos was with a group of men, some young like him, but most of them middle-aged. They were all shirtless and wore long, dark pants, their faces boiled red by the heat. They walked back and forth, back and forth, hefting concrete blocks out of the back of a small truck, carrying them up a hill, then dumping them in a pile at the top. I shivered, despite the heat, imagining the rough concrete blocks cutting into Christos's gentle hands.

I told Katerina what I'd seen. "Yes, those boys work so hard here." She shook her head. "How lucky for Christos to have you at the end of the day!"

Her light tone frustrated me. This was serious. "Is that the only job for him here? Doesn't he go to school?"

"Christos? Maybe he will go to school." She shrugged. "Or maybe he will never leave the island and just build houses like his father. It doesn't matter."

"Of course it matters!" I said.

She looked annoyed. "Why do you think about this, Sarah? You are here. He is here. The sun is warm, the beach is nice, you have a warm man in your bed. Why do you worry every minute?"

That night I told Christos that I had seen him at work. He shrugged. I opened my mouth to say something supportive and kind, but he put his index finger over my lips and shook his head, pulling me to him.

The next day, at the beach, Katerina pointed at the sea. "Look! There is Kostas!" Far from the shore, something black and round bobbed in the water. Then a hand shot up, waving. We waved back.

"He is our friend," she said. "He came this morning from a nearby island."

"On a ferry? You mean the strike is over?"

Katerina shook her head, looking hurt. "No. His uncle has a fishing boat."

We watched Kostas swimming away from us until it was difficult to see him at all. "Is it safe to swim so far out?" I asked.

"Oh, he's not swimming," Katerina said. "He is finding our dinner."

His head disappeared. I stared at the spot where he had been, waiting for him to resurface. Time crawled by. Had he been underneath for just one minute or five? I was about to say something to Katerina when he surfaced with a small wriggling fish at the end of a spear. He swam back to the beach, walked out of the sea, tossed the fish in a bucket, and waded back into the water to repeat the whole process, over and over. Each time his head disappeared, I held my breath until it reappeared. Each time I was convinced that he had stayed down too long. When he had filled his bucket with fish and put down his spear, I felt dizzy and grateful.

"What if he runs out of breath?" I asked Katerina. "What if he gets trapped below the water?"

Katerina smiled and yelled to Kostas. "Sarah thinks the sea is going to eat you, Kostas!"

Kostas sat down next to me on the sand. "Do not worry," he said. "I was born by the sea. I am like a fish."

That evening, Markos and Kostas skinned the fish and fried them in olive oil. We sat eating at a table outside the bar, taking turns making toasts with glasses of ouzo.

"To rich tourists who drink too much!" Markos said.

"To beautiful women with no morals!" said Takis, Markos's friend from Athens.

"To good friends!" Katerina said, winking at me.

"*Yeia sas! Yeia sas!*" we all said, clinking our glasses together.

Kostas said nothing, but smiled and raised his glass to the rest of us. I had made a point of sitting next to him, but suddenly felt too shy to talk to him. He seemed older than we were, although I don't think he was. He turned to me. "Katerina said you are American. I like American literature very much. Truman Capote is my favorite," he said. "You know his books?"

I hesitated. "A little bit," I lied, wishing I had read more. "Did you read Capote in college?"

He smiled, as if at a child who had asked a silly question. "College is not for me. You should try Capote."

I nodded, then tried to change the subject. "What do you do on your island?"

"The same as here," he said, "Fishing, talking with friends, eating . . ."

"But what do you do for work? For a job?"

He told me that he repaired fishing boats. "I help my father," he said. "It is very simple. I do not work so hard."

"But . . . don't you want to do something else?"

"Something else?"

"Well, maybe go to school or get a job that is more . . ."

Kostas examined his beer. "You know, we have so many tourists coming to visit our islands. Germans, French, Swedish. The people from the northern countries, they work so hard. All year long, they just work." He looked up at the evening sky, shaking his head. "And then, they come here, for one week each year, and sit on the beach all day, and drink too much, and their white skin is burned because they are not accustomed to sun. Then they go home and go back to more work." I thought he must resent tourists invading his island and feel impatient with my silly questions, but he didn't seem angry. He just looked sad. Then he looked me in the eyes, with an intensity that caught me off guard. "*That* is not a good life, Sarah. *This* is a good life. This is all I want: fishing, eating with my friends. It is simple, but it is good. You know?"

I nodded, as if I understood. But I didn't. I was confused.

"And you? What do you do, in America?" he asked.

"I don't know," I said without thinking, surprised to realize that this was true. For the first time in my life, I had no plan, no goal, no structure.

Kostas nodded his approval and raised his glass to me. "*Yeia sas.*"

I blushed under his praise, but I still wasn't convinced. His world, like Katerina's, was so alluring, yet so strange. I felt like a ship torn free of its moorings, tossed to and fro by playful gods over sunlit but unpredictable seas. I left the bar early that night, telling Katerina I had a headache.

The next day the strike ended. A boat would arrive in two days. I was determined to be on it. I had been on the island for two weeks. So much had happened, it felt like two months. I announced my departure that night at the bar. Katerina made an exaggerated show of sulking. "How can I live alone here without you?" she wondered aloud. Christos got drunk. Kostas got quiet.

"Why so much hurry?" Markos said. "Your airplane leave soon?"

Everyone looked at me. Even the shy local boys looked right at me, waiting for me to answer. One of them leaned close to me, asking a question over and over that I couldn't understand. He was drunk and spit when he talked, looking angry and gesturing to Katerina, then to Christos, then to the sky. No one translated for me. They didn't need to.

I had planned to lie, to invent a deadline that couldn't be moved, a commitment I had to keep. But there were no deadlines. My flight didn't leave for a month, and even that could be changed.

I had no answer. They turned away and continued drinking.

My last day, we all went to the beach. Even Christos and the other local boys took the day off to join us.

Katerina pointed to them. "Now you see how we love you?" she said.

We lay on the sand and watched Kostas and Markos catch fish. Their heads would disappear at the same time, but Markos always reappeared first. Time stretched into long, wincing moments while I waited to see Kostas's head pop up again, always with the biggest fish on the end of his spear. When they joined us on the beach, I asked Kostas why he stayed underwater so long. "Is it really necessary?"

"I must go very far down," he said. "The best fish are deep, very deep."

Katerina and Markos went swimming. Christos and the local boys joined them. I was happy to be left alone with Kostas. When he was around, I felt calm. I found myself wanting to be near him, not like a lover but like a groupie, a disciple, a doting younger sister.

We watched the others swim away from the shore, beyond the shelter of the cove, until I could barely see their heads among the waves. Their laughter bounced across the water. They waved and called to us. "Let us join them," Kostas said. "The view of the island is very nice out there."

"Are you sure it's safe?"

Kostas smiled. "Sarah, you live like the sky will fall on your head."

"Well, maybe it will. If I'm not careful."

"No," he said, looking out at the water. "Not today. Not here." He stood and reached for my hand.

We swam out so far, I was afraid we would never get back. I was sure some hidden current would sweep us away, out into the Mediterranean, where we'd drown like the ancient mariners who had angered Poseidon.

"Look!" Katerina said when we reached the others. I spun around. I could see the entire island, rising like a dark whale out of the sea, its black cliffs menacing to the outsider, protective of its treasures: at one end, the town—a brilliant streak of white ringed by silver olive groves; across the rest of the island, little white squares dotted the landscape—the farmhouses where the world's best yogurt was made. I could even see the cliff where I'd stood that first morning, looking out at the sea, feeling the island's magic.

That afternoon, I returned my ticket. I stayed another week, letting my plans dissolve like sea salt, my worries hushed by Christos's warm hands, Kostas's gentle lectures, and Katerina's melodramatic devotion. By the time I left, I could no longer recall why I had ever wanted to leave.

On my last night, we said our goodbyes at the bar. Christos shocked me with a gift: a cheap gold charm in the shape of a butterfly. Its tackiness broke my heart. His eyes were red and puffy. Surely it was from some dust in his eyes? He waved away my awkward thank-yous, kissed my cheek, and told me to "remember Greece!"

Katerina refused to say goodbye, insisting on escorting me to my boat at daybreak. "I love you the most," she said, "so I will take you." Kostas looked on with a wry smile from a bench in the corner, his arms folded primly over his chest. As on previous nights, he was the only one of us not drunk. I got up the nerve to sit next to him and . . . what? Thank him? Ask for his blessing? Tell him I'd never forget what he'd taught me? I didn't quite understand it myself. He didn't make me weak in the knees the way Christos did. I just wanted him around the next time I lost my way. I had no idea if he knew this. Like a guru or prophet, he was both irresistible and impervious to praise. He would have laughed—kindly, perplexed—if I had found words to express what I felt. So I just raised my glass to his. "To the good life," I said. His face cracked into a wide smile. "*Yeia sas*," he said.

On the stone pier in the pink light of another dawn, Katerina clung to my hand, glaring at the ferry and its crew. "I can't believe you leave me alone with all those boys," she said. I didn't quite believe it either. After weeks of trying to leave, I wanted to stay, to climb back up the dark cliff, to stay forever on this enchanted island that had produced such delightful and unexpected gifts: a friend, a lover, a teacher. It seemed impossible I'd ever be this lucky, this special, again.

"I refuse to cry," Katerina said, winking at me. "I will wait to be alone, and then I will weep, very bitterly. But you must go. There is another lonely Greek boy waiting for you on the next island, I think." She laughed, then gripped my shoulders and was serious again. "But do not replace me with another girlfriend, okay?" And then I was on the boat, pulling out into the fog, and Katerina was getting smaller and smaller, standing straight and solemn with her head held high, like royalty.

It was five years before I had any contact with Greece. Back home, I had finished college and landed my first real job when I got a letter from Katerina. She was living in America, not far from me. I went to visit her right away.

Dressed in a red bikini top and blue leather pants, she still looked like too much fun. She chopped cucumbers and feta for our lunch. "Just like Greece, right?" she winked at me. Katerina told me she had come to America to become a chiropractor. When she talked about it, her eyes lit up with the same passion she had once had for her little bar with no customers. "It is the future of medicine!"

Things hadn't worked out with Markos. They closed the bar and left the island. "No customers, so what can we do?!" she laughed, handing me a beer. When I asked about Christos, she said she didn't know. She hadn't visited the island in years.

"What about Kostas?"

"Oh, Markos's friend who came to fish?" She put down her knife. "I'm afraid he has died." She took a swig from her beer. "It is very sad. They tell me he is drowned. While spearfishing. He went too deep. The other boys tried to save him, but he just went too deep."

I never saw Katerina after that short visit. When I wrote her a few months later, the letters came back. I try to imagine her now, somewhere in Greece, wearing a white lab coat over a low-cut shirt, adjusting spines and breaking hearts. I think of Christos, still living on the island, still hauling bricks. By now he has married one of the invisible local girls; perhaps on his days off, he takes his young children to the beach. Then I think of Kostas. *I was right after all*, I think. *The sky* did *fall.* But then I hear his voice, and I feel better: *Do not worry, Sarah. I am like a fish.*

Last, I imagine a young American girl on her own for the first time. She is lonely, cautious, and thinks she has thought of everything. But then she takes a risk and finds her way to a small island that everyone else has missed, where things happen that she could not have planned. She is never quite the same again.

Alison Cadbury

The *Folitsa*

The house was not at all what I expected. I stood, astonished, in the dusty road beside the landmark—a large stand of prickly pear, its lobes thrusting out bristly nubbins. It was mid-March. Above me, the hills and fields of the island were greening; below, the surface of the Aegean rippled like midnight-blue crepe de chine. From orchards between the sea and the house, gentle breezes carried the sharp, sweet scent of lemon blossoms.

I had walked two miles (*two cigarettes*, by Greek country measure) from the main town of the island of Paros to look at a country house to rent for the summer. An hour or two before, I had met the owner, one Kosmas, at a coffeehouse. He treated me to a lemonade and watched me carefully through lizard eyes. He gave me a large iron key and told me, "Pass the chapel on the hill, pass the ruins of the Asklipion, then one more cigarette, and there you are. Are you a good housekeeper?"

"*Etsi k'etsi*," I answered. "So-so." He grunted and waved me off. Kosmas wore a perfectly fitted black dress suit and snowy white shirt. Whatever he once had been, he now was old, old and tiny. He seemed to have shrunk without becoming either bent or wrinkled. His small skull, showing only wisps of white hair beneath his black cap, seemed too frail to support the nose that protruded like an eagle's beak. His lashless eyes were lidded like those of a gecko, but sparkled with humor, even devilry. I had seen him earlier that winter at a saint's day party. It was almost three in the morning when he had risen from the table, placed a glass of retsina on his bald head and danced a few steps, catching the glass before it fell, and draining it to great applause. "*Yero potiri!*" the guests had called, "Strong glass!"—praise for a good drinker.

I was elated to get out of the town, shake off the chill and dankness of a winter spent overdressed in heavy clothes that seemed never to dry out. For months I had huddled in unheated tavernas with terrazzo floors whose iciness penetrated boots and rose to the knees, stiffening as it went. I wanted heat, I wanted sunshine, I wanted the amniotic sea, and, most of all, I wanted solitude. I had a book to write.

Kosmas's age and frailty eased a concern I shared with other foreigners about renting houses on the island. The Greeks did not seem to share our notions of privacy. A room retained by the owner for "storage" would suddenly, around Easter or the feast of the Assumption, become lodging for half a dozen relatives for a few weeks. A German couple I knew arrived home at a remote, rented country house one winter day to find several sheep quartered in an unused room. This led to words and involved the police, who weighed in on the side of the shepherd: The room was empty; the sheep needed a place to sleep, why not?

Minor, but mysterious, trespasses occurred frequently at the house I had been renting in town. Strange laundry would appear on my balcony one morning; the next morning, my own wash, hung out the evening before, would vanish only to be seen waving gaily from a neighboring balcony, which led me to believe that the sweet old lady next door had stolen all my underwear. That the underwear would be returned, dried, ironed, and even mended did not help the confusion about *meum et tuum*. Worse, some landlords seemed to feel that single women—poor, lonely things—were renting not so much space as "company." However, Kosmas's ninety-some years and the distance from the town seemed to guarantee the privacy I sought.

Key in pocket, I set out. Above the road the low, toast-colored mountains stepped down to the sea in ancient stone-walled terraces holding fields of wheat and vegetables, orchards of olives and figs, and vineyards. Below, near the sea, flatter fields were planted in melons, tomatoes, and eggplants, while high-walled orchards held back the wind from orange and pomegranate trees.

It was a perfect day: The fields blazed green with ripening wheat and crimson with poppies. Snowy white houses peeped from among the dark green leaves of citrus and the silver-green of olives. Here and there a late-blooming almond tree scattered its pink blossoms in the sea breeze. Below them all, visible from every house, the sea in all its amazing shades, jade to sapphire to amethyst, stretched out to the horizon.

As I walked, I dreamed of my perfect Cycladic house. The hillsides were dotted with clusters of farmhouses and their box-shaped barns, stables, coops, cheese-making rooms, and dove towers, the roofs stepping down from terrace to terrace. In their new Easter whitewash, they shone brilliantly against the treeless, stony, pale terra-cotta hillside, looking from afar like assemblages of children's building blocks made of feta cheese. I longed to live in one and learn the ways of country life: hauling water from a well, baking in a beehive oven, doing laundry in a stone *skafi*, or washtub.

But Kosmas's house was not the plain rectangle of white-washed stone with blue windows celebrated by Le Corbusier and Gropius and sought after by artistic foreigners like myself. Far from being a traditional, it was someone's idea of a posh, urbane dwelling rendered, not very competently, in native materials and techniques. A straight path led through a small vineyard to a gateway of two not-quite-plumb stone columns surmounted by a triangular pediment, not carved from marble but cobbled together out of island slate. This entrance opened onto a wide flagstone terrace, sheltered from the road by pink oleander bushes.

The rectangular facade of the house was divided symmetrically: On either side, a large window and a sculpture niche framed the front door, which told the story. Over three meters high, the heavily molded and grilled double door with a brass knocker, in the shape of a woman's hand, belonged not to a small country house on an island but to a neoclassical house in a city. Someone, I conjectured, had been to Athens and seen those elegant mid-nineteenth-century houses, said, "That's for me," returned to the island, and duplicated one.

I unlocked the door and entered to find more evidence of urbanity: ceramic tile floors. In the *saloni*, or living room, the floor imitated a carpet: cream with rust and gray ribbons threading along the verges and tied in a bowknot in the middle. The floor of the kitchen was classic black-and-white checkerboard—but, as I opened the outside door, I noticed on the threshold a single white tile with a red heart at its center.

The house proved to be perfect for writing. The romantic novel I was writing was set in both Athens and the island, and the odd little house seemed to echo both settings. I quickly established a routine: I woke up early, drank my Nescafé on the terrace, read over the previous day's work, and wrote some more. About ten or eleven, I went to the beach for a vigorous swim and returned to lunch on the tomatoes and cheese I had bought from the neighbors, Ilias and Maria. In the blazing afternoons, I napped and then went down to the cove for another swim. The Greek nights were as warm as a velvet wrap, so I ate supper outside, sitting sometimes in brilliant moonlight, sometimes in the blue-ink dark, breathing in the scents of sharp eucalyptus and sweet Pancratium lilies and listening to the owls.

For two weeks, I lived in heaven. I was finally at home. My writing flowed like an artesian spring. Then, shortly after dawn one morning, I was awakened by something prodding me through the sheets. I opened my eyes with a start to see first his cane and then Kosmas, straw-hatted and sturdily booted. He was, it seemed, not only a strong glass but a strong foot.

"Wake up, lazy girl," he demanded, "and make me a coffee!" Startled, to say the least, I was reviewing my opinion of his harmlessness, when he tactfully went down to the garden to let me dress. He had brought Greek coffee and some freshly baked koulourakia, sweet biscuits. Still wary, I (never the perfect housewife) hastened to wash a couple of cups and put the *briki*, Greek coffee pot, on to boil. After one sip, Kosmas dumped his coffee and mine down the drain and carefully instructed me in the proper way to prepare it. "So when I come, you'll know," he said.

It sank in that he was planning multiple visits, and I must have looked a little apprehensive, because he laughed and said, "Don't worry! I'm ninety-four and . . ." a graphic gesture with his forefinger indicated that he no longer had a need for a girlfriend. So what had he come for?

It took me three or four nervous visits to realize that Kosmas came to talk about his wife. On the *saloni* wall hung a photograph, a somewhat faded portrait of a dark matronly woman of considerable embonpoint. This was his wife. He always called her *i kyria mou*, my lady, never *i gynaika mou*, my woman, as the other island men did. Nor did he call her by name. She had died twenty years ago, and he still missed her terribly. He never told me much; mostly he would drink his coffee, stare at the portrait, and talk about the weather or the neighbors. But I learned gradually that they had lived together in this house for almost fifty years. They had no children. After she died, he moved to town to live with his widowed sister.

I reminded Kosmas of his wife; he compared me to her often, pointing out in the portrait the dark, abundant hair, the large eyes ("though hers were as black as olives," he sighed), the square jaw, and the wide mouth. Among the attributes we seemed to have in common was that she had been, surprisingly, a great swimmer. Early one June morning, Kosmas walked in with my bathing suit hanging from the tip of his cane. "Shame! Hanging your underwear out in front!"

"That's my bathing suit," I answered grumpily.

"So little?" he said. I knew what he meant; Greek women's bathing suits I had seen on the beach could have upholstered sofas. "Anyway, you shouldn't hang clothes out at night; bad spirits can get in them." The suit reminded him of how his wife would go swimming: "Every day," he sighed, "from April to December, she went down to the sea, by herself. Such a woman! An Amazon!" I thought she must have been; such athleticism was unusual in young Greek island women in the early seventies, much less middle-aged ones.

In the photo she looked a little grim, but this was not so in life: "She was a great laugher," he would sigh, "very witty. She could tell jokes . . . and make up verses to the wedding songs—always the most shocking!"

Shocking (*tsoking*) means bawdy. At the memory of her bawdiness, Kosmas would wipe away a tear with his sleeve. "It was for her I bought this picture," he said as he pointed to it with his cane, "because she was a poet, too." The picture was a nineteenth-century painting of a very elongated lady in a transparent chiton with tiny feet and hands, and enormous thighs, lolling in a boat somewhat too small for her and waving a script about the size of a shopping list. In the background was a misty temple. Painted in a lozenge on the frame was the name Sappho.

All the comparisons were not positive. "*Ach,* you're a dirty girl," he would complain. "My lady kept these floors shining like glass." Or, "You are no housewife; you never have any food in the house, just canned things and macaroni. Are you dieting?" Once he brought me a paper cone of tiny silver fish. With heads. And scales. I had no idea what to do with them. When he left, I fed them to the cats. They were ecstatic, not being fond of my macaroni scraps.

I grew used to Kosmas's early-morning visits, even looked forward to them, though dawn was never my time and we conversed about little else than his wife and the weather. Once, after two weeks had passed without sign of him, I mentioned his absence to Ilias and Maria, who were distant relatives, while I was buying vegetables. "He's not ill, is he?"

"Kosmas? Not him!" Maria laughed, "He's gone to Naxos for a baptism. He'll be back when the party's over!" Strong glass.

Between visits, I pursued my idyllic life, discovering more and more delights of the odd little house. The windows not only admitted light but framed beautiful and peaceful views: The *saloni* window opened onto an olive grove where I could see little olives turning from green to blue among the silver-green leaves, while the window opposite my bed framed a view of a field with a huge bushy fig tree. The cow who was pastured there was extremely fond of figs; day by day, she nuzzled the leaves and branches, stretching higher and higher to reach the figs, rearing up her great bulk on unsteady legs and, with eyes closed in ecstasy, feasting on the highest—and sweetest—of the figs. I enjoyed visits with Ilias and Maria and another farmer, Vassilis, who sold me vegetables and fruit and great bunches of green leafy basil. Once when I asked Vasilis for a second bunch, planning to make pesto for friends, he lifted a sardonic, gray eyebrow and said, "What are you doing with so much basil—eating it?"

"Of course," I said, puzzled.

"*Mor-e*," he expostulated, "Basil is a *flower!*" He gave it to me anyway and, afterward, would call across the field, "Still eating flowers? How about some zinnias?"

I would be wrong to say that the spirit of Kosmas's wife haunted the house or that I felt it much. I had my own life, a happy one. My writing was going well, I was strong and healthy, I had a lover or two and friends who enjoyed walking out and surprising me with a midnight picnic. And yet sometimes, when I was washing dishes in the brown marble sink, I would realize it had been built a bit lower than usual, for the comfort of a woman exactly my height. Once, coming in from a moonlit swim and passing her portrait, I even spoke to her: "Tonight, the sea was as warm as my skin. It was the most extraordinary sensation! Did you ever?"

Sometimes, too, stuck for a word or a thought, I would think of her making up scandalous verses and could almost hear her hearty laughter. And yet, stepping across the heart on the kitchen threshold, I at times wondered whether all this love the old man showed was only an afterthought, the nostalgia of loneliness.

One afternoon around the feast of the Assumption in mid-August, I came home from the beach to find a middle-aged woman setting out a picnic on the stone table on my terrace. Three or four children milled around, trying to sneak the cookies she was arranging on a plate. My plate. Seeing me, she cried out, "Oh, here you are! Welcome!" She introduced herself as Kosmas's niece, Annio, and the children as his grandnieces and -nephews. To a dark-haired little boy, Kosmakis (little Kosmas), she said, "Tell your mother to hurry with the coffee. She's here, *i kseni mas*," (our foreigner), an epithet between a compliment and an oxymoron. Another child emerged with some forks and a knife.

"Do you know how to gather prickly pears?" asked Annio, leading me up the path to the stand of cacti, now sprouting orange-red fruits with fearsome spines. I knew they were edible, but a traumatic experience with the thorns had put me off further efforts. Talking all the time, she speared the fruits with a fork, sliced thorns off with the knife, then peeled off the skin without touching it. She offered me a slice on the point of a knife. "Sweet?"

"Delicious," I said, still surprised by the invasion and hoping they were not here for a long stay. We cut a few more prickly pears then went back to the terrace where her sister was pouring coffee.

"Kosmas told us about you," Annio said, feeding a cookie to a little girl. "You remind him of his wife."

"Did you know her?"

"Oh, of course! Auntie Chryssoula?" This was the first time I had heard her name. Maro, the second niece, fed the children and sent them into the garden to strip all the fruit off the trees— overripe plums, green lemons, green almonds. Annio and I settled down for a good gossip.

I was curious about when and why the house had been built. It puzzled me that there was only one bedroom and, unlike the native houses, no way to build on more, as it was built almost to the property line on each side and so in-filled in back that an addition would have been structurally impossible. "Ah, Uncle Kosmas, he had money," Annio said, rubbing her fingers together, "and could have anyone. Auntie was just a farmer's daughter, but he only wanted her. Then, five years and they had no children. But it didn't spoil the marriage. Not for them. But the village . . . you know . . . *muzz-muzz*. Sly looks. Auntie missed the country anyway, so what did he do but build her a house out here! But such a house! A little palace it was then. And here they lived for fifty years, like lovers. *Folitsa*," she sighed, a nest. A love nest, a pretty and elegant solace, with that heart on the threshold.

Maro came out of the house, carrying a big canvas bag, and the two sisters attacked the prickly pear. After a few minutes, to my relief, they were on their way to visit neighbors. I went inside to find all the dishes washed, the floors swept, and three peeled prickly pears on a plate under a napkin. I didn't begrudge the lemons.

I never found out what Chryssoula died of; I'm sure it was something cataclysmic, swift and sudden, because I cannot believe the woman I had in some way come to know would weaken and deteriorate. Nor had her Kosmas. He had not ceased to live and enjoy life, but neither had he ceased to grieve. "I have a hole in my heart," he said once, "and in it is an icon of her, with a flame before it."

As winter came on, the fierce north winds turned the high-ceilinged house into a refrigerator, and drenching rains transformed the road to town into a river with rapids, discouraging visitors. I gave up the house and moved into town. I often saw Kosmas sitting among the old men outside the grocery store or in coffeehouses. He would hail me and I would sit and drink a coffee with him.

"Better than your coffee," he would laugh. On festival days, in the tavernas, he was always part of a large party and, as usual, holding up his reputation as a "strong glass."

The following summer I moved to a remote farmhouse on the other, less populated side of the island. There on the top of a small mountain I finally had my traditional Cycladic house, complete with earth floors, beehive oven, and a bed under which wheat was stored. It had a view of both the rising moon and the setting sun, and somewhat distant neighbors from whom I learned many things about the earthbound, native life of the islands. But in my heart too is a little icon of tiny Kosmas and his Amazon of a wife, framed in the pedimented doorway of the house built for love.

Liza Monroy

Going Home to Greece

The year I started college in Boston, my mother packed up and moved to Greece, her fifth assignment of her U.S. Foreign Service career, yet another move in her spunky-divorcée-doing-something-crazy life. Thanks to her job, I had been raised in Mexico, Italy, and other countries. Greece was the first move she made without me, her daughter-in-tow. When I visited her there, I did so as an adult. Greece for us was neutral territory, past countries and memories left far behind.

I was intrigued by the wonders of Greece, its tradition as a mythological land with striking white temples and the beauty of the Aegean Sea, by its place in history as the birthplace of Western philosophy and the society responsible for countless advancements of civilization. Also, to a college student, the Greek islands sounded like the perfect summer party destination. I couldn't wait to go and couldn't wait to tell my college friends that I was heading *home* to Athens for the holiday break.

I read everything I could about the country, even revisiting an old mythology text I'd studied in high school. I thought of my relationship with my mother while thumbing the pages of one well-known myth; she was like Demeter, and now that I was pulling away into my own, she was searching for the daughter who had gone into the underworld, inhabiting a different realm, dictating the seasons for herself. At nineteen, I was convinced that I was Persephone, hiding in Hades and not sure I even wanted to come out.

The Boston Common was covered in seven inches of snow that mid-December day I flew to Greece. When I got off the plane in Athens, it wasn't exactly hot, but the air was light and easy to breathe. The sun shone with a crystalline quality I had never seen anywhere else. No wonder travel articles about Greece always mentioned the light.

"*Yeia sou!*" my mother said as she greeted me at the airport. *So she is Greek already,* I thought.

"*Yeia sou, mitera,*" I replied, remembering the handful of words she'd taught me out of her language text.

My mother's apartment was in Glyfada, a thirty-minute drive up the coast from the city, depending on the traffic along the national highway, which ranged from pretty bad to bumper-to-bumper unbearable. But the road ran along the sea. My mom always kept a swimsuit and towel in the back of the little red Honda del Sol convertible she'd imported from Washington, D.C., where she'd studied Greek before commencing her tour of duty. After work, she would sometimes drive past the exit to her apartment building and head for Voula Beach, where she'd change from her work clothes and into her bathing suit, and run into the Impressionist painting that was the Aegean at sunset—flecks of pink and orange dancing over the lazily shifting water. Late August and early September—when the sun's warmth lessened, but not the water's—were the perfect months for an evening swim. By then, tourists were trickling home, receding like the waves as the sun fell behind the distant horizon.

We took the top off the car, and Mom, her blond, highlighted hair blowing in the wind, sped through the *chaos* (I now know why we got this word from the Greek) of Greek drivers toward Glyfada. Her apartment was two blocks from the beach, and if you stood on the balcony and craned your neck, you could glimpse a sliver of the sea. Mom had decided I should take in the town, which I had heard referred to as "the Beverly Hills of Athens."

"A frappé at the *kafenio* will cure your jet lag right away," she said.

"What's that?" I asked. "Sounds like a milkshake."

"It's the strongest coffee you'll ever taste," she said, her light brown eyes glinting. I wasn't a big coffee drinker at the time, but to this day I blame the Greek frappé for my javaddiction.

The *kafenio* is ubiquitous in Glyfada; there seemed to be several on every block, all with outdoor seating on garden patios or spilling onto the sidewalk. My mother ordered two frappés, *parakalo;* and when the waiter brought them, she said, *"Efharisto poli,"* and made small talk with him in her shockingly fluent Greek. She told me she had a Greek boyfriend and was contemplating buying property near Voula Beach. She had even bought a motorcycle, which sat gathering dust in her garage.

"So what are we going to do while I'm here?" I asked, newly wide awake and buzzing from the potent mix of Nescafé, water, and sugar.

"We're going skiing," said my mother.

"But I only just got here," I said, imagining she'd planned for us to jet off to the Swiss Alps before I even got a chance to explore my new home.

"We're not flying anywhere," she explained. "We're skiing right here in Greece."

"You can ski in *Greece?*" I hadn't read about that in my guidebook, which covered mostly islands with blue and white buildings, hikes in Crete, and how to get to the Parthenon.

"There's a mountain in the town of Arachova, Mount Parnassos."

Arachova was only two hours away, near Delphi, home of the famous oracle. I couldn't believe that the dampness of white powder and the whoosh of skis were so close to the warmth of the Aegean Sea.

My mother had secretly been plotting to retire from the foreign service and live in Greece. She had been searching for the perfect place to settle, and nowhere had been quite right—until now. On the way to Arachova, she pulled over on the highway to show me the plot of land she hoped to buy, land on which she would build her long-awaited dream house. It was a smallish patch of land on a hill. We climbed the grassy slope, the cool breeze blowing through our hair, and stood on the property, looking out over the ocean sparkling below, flecks of sun like Poseidon's jewels shimmering over the surface. *Is this it?* I wondered. *Could we have found home— a real one?*

"Can you imagine a little house right here?" she asked. Her *house* had always been something we talked about in an abstract, future tense. I could imagine it, but I also didn't believe it. Gypsies didn't settle down, much less buy property.

We arrived in Arachova in the late afternoon and strolled along the town's cobblestone streets lined with little shops selling multicolored bottles of locally produced honey, wine, and candied fruits. Sausages hung suspended in windows. Sheep grazed on majestic expanses of nearby hills. An afternoon symphony of clanging bells rang out hourly from the town clock tower. Although the clock chimed the hour, the Greeks in this popular ski town seemed to possess a disregard for time. Young people vibrantly chatted in the outdoor *kafenio*. As night fell, we found a taverna, where we sipped homemade wine and ordered souvlaki.

After dinner, we wandered around looking for a bar where we could have a nightcap. Arachova's watering holes were dotted with gray heads of men gliding their backgammon pieces quickly across the tables.

"There aren't any other women in here," I said. "Let's try another place," said my mom. Yet each bar was the same—all men, no women. We finally just sat down.

"They come to escape the wife, but you can never really escape her for that long," the bartender remarked when we asked about the customers. My mother and I raised our eyebrows at one another and ordered a carafe of red wine. We were surrounded by clicking, sliding, dice-falling sounds as the Greek men played backgammon. I knew the game well; my college roommate Marissa was obsessed and insisted I not only learn it, but become adept, investing hours upon hours of practice. I fell behind on guitar, but I was a champ at the game I'd once considered obscure. I hadn't known it was the national game of Greece (and its rival Turkey as well).

I smiled at one of the more grandfatherly types and gestured the question of whether I could play. He laughed and pulled up a chair from a nearby table. No one thought I stood a chance. With each throw of the dice, we calculated expert moves. My throws were good: a four and six, a two and four—random tosses that allowed me to make lots of little short stacks with my backgammon pieces, a strategy Marissa had taught me. The old man and I began pulling our pieces off the board around the same time. What I loved most about the game was that it was impossible to tell who was winning until the very end, when somebody actually won. This was the closest game I'd ever played. Some men gathered around, looking on in surprise.

"Go Liza!" said my mother, ever the enthusiastic cheerleader.

We were down to about ten pieces each. It was crunch time, win or lose. The next couple of rolls would determine everything.

Then it happened: I rolled double sixes—the player's ultimate hope, the best break from chance or fate, whichever you chose to believe. (The Greeks seemed to favor the latter.) I won.

The dismayed, de-machofied local bought us a second carafe of wine, perhaps more to reclaim his masculinity than a gift to the winner. If there was anything Greek men were territorial about, it was backgammon; they deemed themselves incredibly skilled, and to be beaten by a woman . . . well, let's just say we proved our worth in their typically male-dominant worldview. My mother slapped me a high-five and poured some of our wine in the man's cup. We toasted, and any bad feelings he had about his loss to an American teenager were forgotten.

On the slopes the following day, the snow was light and powdery. Music blared over outdoor speakers as we zipped down the mountain. It could have been the Alps, the Dolomites, or the Tetons. I still could not believe I was skiing a few hours outside of Athens. It couldn't have felt farther away from Glyfada, where the sun sank over the sea in hues of orange and azure.

Back home, which Glyfada had now become, we tried to decide on a taverna for dinner. After a week in Greece, I'd come to expect the standard fare: souvlaki, *taramosalata, dolmades, horiatiki salata,* calamari. We decided to try the fancy Chinese restaurant across the street from the apartment, which turned out to be the best Chinese food I ever tasted.

When I flew back to Boston the following week, I realized I felt at home in Greece and, like Persephone in the springtime, was emerging from my winter funk. I had also attained a peaceful closeness with my mother. The chance to travel with her, without being bound to moving all the time as her daughter-in-tow, was liberating. Greece was the ideal place for her to settle down; this land of passion, of history, of mythology was a place I'd be satisfied to call—at long last—home.

After spending the second semester of my sophomore year abroad in the Netherlands, I flew back to Greece. This time I could swim in the ocean—skiing was not on the agenda. My mother and I headed south on a night ferry to Skala, a port town on Patmos.

We rented a motorcycle from an old man in a shop near the port and rode toward the cave called the Holy Grotto of the Revelation. My mother was in the driver's seat and I clutched her weight, my head turned to the right, encased by a clunky white helmet. Patmos was still and calm; the only sounds were the puttering engine of our *motorino* and the clanging of Grecian sheeps' bells off in the distance. It was a time for reflection, another retreat into stillness, far from the ebb and flow of the course of modern life.

In AD 95, according to history books, the Revelation of Saint John the theologian happened in a cave on Patmos, where John spent the duration of his eighteen-month exile. A monastery stands there today. The grotto is a major destination for pilgrims from around the world. *If I were stuck in a cave for more than a year,*

I might start hearing the voice of God, too, I thought, until I read in my guidebook that John is the patron saint of booksellers, at which point I lowered my eyes and silently prayed for the future of my novel, still a seed in my brain.

On the way to the cave, we stopped in a tiny, typical hillside church. A small, old lady shrouded in black waved incense in the air. She smiled toothlessly, her eyes squinting and reflecting off the light streaming in through the entryway.

"There's something mystical about the Greek Orthodox religion, isn't there?" I wondered aloud, as I stared at the gold paintings and inhaled the old woodsy scent of the woman's incense holder, the candles burning in their red glass holders.

"It's very mystical," said my mother.

I imagined Gregorian chants echoing through the tiny, dark chapel. But the only sound was that of waves crashing against the cliffs below. We emerged back into the daylight and on to our trusty *motorino.*

"Can I drive?" I asked.

"No," she said, her fist already twisting the handlebar, starting up the bike. I rolled my eyes and swung my leg over the back. I guess I was still the child in some ways.

As we entered the dim, silent cave, I realized the source of this feeling of mysticism. It struck me like my very own revelation. The island's geography, the natural spirituality within the quiet stone walls, and the cobalt hues of the ocean below all seemed to erase the complications of daily life. It was the perfect moment in the perfect place to just be, and to connect—or reconnect—with another person. The cave felt like a retreat back to a slower time, when people lived close to nature and had time for contemplation.

The next day, we went to the smaller town of Kampos, then rode over to Psili Ammos, the nude beach, which was a safe distance from the monastery. I lay naked in the sun reading Ovid's *Metamorphoses.* I imagined the dark-robed monks up the hill and the nude hippies in the ocean were connected despite being such opposites, like figures in an Escher etching. Then I wrote in my journal, *My mother and I are true opposites. I'm defined by reflection, thought, writing. She opens her mouth and just lets things spill out, like* gigantes *(large Greek beans) pouring from a jar.*

In the end, my mother didn't make an offer on that swatch of Greek land. Ever the nomad, she decided to just keep going, looking, searching. But my visits to Greece were the first times we saw each other as women, as friends and cohorts. Those were the trips that turned us into two women, who set off on adventures, neither of us in our homeland. She moved on, to Rome, then to Caracas, that house to settle into still talked about in future tense.

Instead of the summer party land I had once imagined, Greece was the beginning of my journey into adulthood, linking the country in my mind to the world to which Persephone returned in Spring, the three Fates weaving my past, present, and future. It was a feeling best defined by a word with Greek roots— *epifania*, epiphany. A sudden intuitive realization—the moment you understand.

Ashley Black

Adespotos

In the mountains of northern Greece, they say you can still find the Sarakatsani.

Semimythical, these aloof nomads are rarely seen in the wild. One only stumbles across an occasional clue. Near Monodhendri, I entered a clearing and found vacated huts in which they had settled for the summer and then vanished. Once, on a mule trail in the Zagoria, I heard a distant barking and the murmur of sheep bells. I followed the sounds to the edge of a dazzling gorge, but there nothing stirred except a floating hawk. Like gods, the Sarakatsani manifest themselves to us mortals in tantalizing glimpses.

They call themselves *Adespoti* (those with no ruler).

To the northwestern wilds, which once thronged with Sarakat-sani, the private investigator had sent me to a village called Phitéa, high in the Mourgana Mountains and so close to the Albanian border that now, as I drove up the gravel road, higher and higher with each spiral, I could make out Greek soldiers on the distant peaks guarding the border.

This is Epirus, a sparse land, mountainous, with sharp, white crags poking so close to the blue sky that you feel you have ascended to a higher plain where only gods and animals dare to live. Scarcity makes life simple, minimalist. Heartbreakingly beautiful, the poets say, and they are right. Up here, the dawn really is rosy-fingered, as Homer claimed, and the magic of an ancient world still persists. In America, we don't have magi who can cast spells, we don't have the Evil Eye. We no longer have nomads who live in tepees. But Greece has not lost its magic.

He said I had been born here, here in this godlike vastness. His Internet name was pomegranate_k. He specialized in finding the birth parents of American children born in Greece. We exchanged emails for a year. I'd given up when he called me to say he had contacted someone who remembered the baby Eleftheria and a family with my birth parents' surname.

I passed a sign, white letters on a scarlet background:

APAGOREUETAI

H LHYH FWTOGRAFIWN

PHOTOGRAPHS

ARE PROHIBITED

Invasion of Greece has been a habit among nations—Turks, Venetians, Genoese, Germans, Italians, and Albanians. The Greek government doesn't want anyone mapping out the routes for another invasion.

My rented car skidded on the gravel as I took a tight turn. For an hour I had been winding my way up these starched plunging ridges, blindingly white in the afternoon sun. For centuries, this road had been a mule trail, used by shepherds and caravans, and had only recently been widened, minimally, for vehicles.

Far below, I saw tiny square patches, green with cucumber and tomato plants or yellow with cornstalks. The Greeks plant every semifertile centimeter of their rocky countryside.

The investigator had told me that the man who remembered my birth parents was a shepherd named *barba* Michas. A shepherd.

So, in my enthusiasm, I had stopped in Metsovo and bought a capote, the traditional calf-length shepherd's cape of thick black goat hair.

I passed a khan, a memento of those days when people traveled by foot, and shepherds who, with their migrating herds, needed a place to spend the night. I had never felt so small. The world around me was vast, eternal, mythic.

And then, smack before me was a film crew. Their vans dangled at the cliff's edge. Cameras focused on what I guessed to be an Athenian rock star, hair dramatically coiffed, makeup liberally administered, nails richly painted. Standing at the edge of a two-hundred-meter drop, she sang a popular Greek song, "To Tango Ti Nefelis." They were making a music video.

I turned the corner, and the anachronistic vision was out of sight. Quickly, I lurched to a dead stop. A middle-aged woman led two lumbering cows across the road. As she crossed in front of my car, the windshield framed her profile, hollow-cheeked and aquiline with a calm, intense set of eyes, something that belonged on a coin in the British Museum.

She herded her animals to a safe perimeter of the road then looked directly at me and raised her palm in greeting. In her modest headscarf, her faded blue dress with its homespun apron, and her shoulder-high walking staff at her side, her gesture bore an understated dignity.

"*Herete, Kyria*" (Greetings, madam), I said.

She gave the slightest nod and spoke, "*Herete sas*" (Greetings to you).

She walked on with her cows, an immortal figure against the grass and schist of the mountain peeks.

I felt foolish, crass, motoring past her up the mountain.

Up ahead were a series of stone buildings, and I thought I had reached Fitia. But it was a ghost village, a series of single-story buildings, walls with stones so carefully placed they had stood without mortar for centuries. The buildings—some with corrugated tin roofs, some unprotected—were scattered haphazardly up and down the slopes. But they only seemed haphazard because they were deserted, and the paths that connected the buildings and gave them context were overgrown. No doors, windows long gone, no stacks of grain or firewood—it was sorrowful.

On a long stone wall, painted in thick red paint, was evidence of the proud perpetrators of this destruction—the hammer and sickle beside the letters KKE. The village had been burned by the Communists, probably during the civil war of 1947–49.

The Greek Civil War. After World War II, when Stalin was spreading his iron curtain around Eastern Europe, Greece hung in the balance. The governments of Yugoslavia and Albania gave supplies and refuge to the Greek Andartes (Communist rebels). Up here the Andartes had made their last stand against the forces of the Greek government. Had my parents died here?

I rounded another shaky curve, and Phitéa came into view. Across a deep ravine, white stone buildings with cheery red tile roofs speckled the hillside and glistened in the long slanting rays of the evening sun.

A single-lane rickety bridge took me across the ravine. The village streets, paved with stones, sloped toward the center to make a gutter. Side streets ran to my right and left, but only the main street was wide enough to risk a car. It took me to the *plateia*.

You find a *plateia*, or town square, in most Greek villages. This one was paved with stone and shaded by a massive plane tree, its roots tapping a subterranean branch of the Styx that fed the handsome stone fountain beside it. I took a drink.

With its wooden benches, small tables, and old men playing *biriba* (Greek gin rummy), the place invited indolence. Along one side of the *plateia* was a *kafenio* (coffee shop) with yellow plastic tables and chairs outside. Two men sat at a table shouting at each other until one slammed his fist on the table. Then they rose, embraced, and bid each other *antio*. One of them wore the white apron of the *kafedzi*, the operator of the *kafenio*.

It was getting late, and I took a table.

"Menu?" the *kafedzi* asked me in English.

"Yes, I should like to eat now," I said in polite Greek.

Few outsiders trouble to learn Greek, and my pathetic efforts earned me an approving nod from the *kafedzi*.

Brimming with self-congratulatory zest, I went on in Greek, "May I see what you have?" This is the custom, to go into the kitchen and see what looks good.

He led me inside and took a pot out of the refrigerator. Beneath the cover he revealed moschari (veal). In another pot, *arnáki* (lamb). Both looked the same, prepared in a tomato pepper sauce. He told me he could also prepare roast goat.

"*Katsíki psitó.*" I ordered the goat sight unseen.

"*Horiatíki?*" Salad.

"*Oréa,*" I said. Beautiful.

The *kafedzi* told me I spoke Greek well. I skipped back to my table, reckless with confidence.

I have read somewhere that the language you hear first is the easiest to learn. On my first trip to Greece, I wasn't aware that I had been born here. But from the time I could read, I had immersed myself in Greece and its singular history—Plato, Aeschylus, Homer, Thucydides. How many times had I read about Thermopylae?

That first trip, that first evening, I had dinner on the roof of my hotel. I opened the menu, but leaned back and stared across the tile roofs of Plaka. I began to cry.

The solicitous waiter rushed to my side. "Miss, Miss . . ." The rest of the staff joined him, arguing heatedly with each other about why this American tourist was crying.

Finally I touched my waiter's gleaming white sleeve and pointed straight ahead. "The Acropolis . . ." I blubbered.

There it stood, the Acropolis with its temple to Athena, gleaming white in the slanting rays of the late summer sun. It shimmered in the heat like an apparition from a much nobler past, which it was.

"Yes, yes," the waiter nodded. And he turned to his companions and said something. All I understood was "to Acropolis." When he turned back to me, there were tears in his eyes, too.

"I have dreamed of seeing the Acropolis," I told him, "all my life." I blew my nose.

He told the others, and one of them said something to me in Greek with a certainty about human nature uniquely Hellenic. My waiter translated, "He says your spirit is Greek."

Not yet aware of having been born in Greece, I only knew that it had been love before sight.

That day, I began studying demotic (modern Greek), and—though for years I have struggled to progress past menu French—I am able to understand Greek. Do I remember it from the womb?

A man in a shepherd's black capote passed close to my table in the *kafenio*. He led a snorting mule which bore the body of a recently slaughtered goat. The *kafedzi* greeted him and the muleteer heaved the carcass over his shoulder and followed the *kafedzi* into the kitchen.

My stomach tightened. I learned reverence for my meal.

Other villagers arrived for dinner and shouted greetings to each other.

The woman I had passed on the road hobbled into the *plateia*, parked her cows by the fountain, and took a seat.

I greeted her again, "*Herete, Kyria.*"

A woman in her forties strode through the *plateia*. She was beautiful in that powerful way often found in older European women. Her hair was pale brown, tousled and short. And she was dressed like a city person in a pale gray dress, simple and crisp.

She was received on every side with affectionate inquiries; she nodded right and left silently in contrast to the booming sociability of her neighbors.

She strode to my table and gestured toward the woman with the cows. "You know Angeliki?" she asked in English. Her eyes, gray-blue and deep, met mine with disconcerting directness.

"I met her on the road on my way here." I was dazzled and stuttered in English.

She interrupted me, "You are the Greek who is lost in America. My father is Michas Tcharikis. I am Athena. What did you order?"

"*Katsiki psito.*"

"*Orea.* It is always very fresh." She called to the *kafedzi*, "Yorgos, *dhio katsiki.*" She sat down and spoke quietly. "It is good you have come. I worry about my father. My mother was taken by

Charon [the god of the underworld] at Pascha [Easter]. He has been very sad. When you say you will come, his spirits were better; he waits with excitement—to meet you."

Athena was a lawyer in Ioannina, but she had been staying with her father since her mother's death.

I was distracted by sheep bells, though there were no sheep in sight, but in this vast landscape, sounds travel for miles, and the tinny tinkle carried as lightly on the air as sunlight across the blue sky. Coming from a distance, so light and clear, the sounds melded together melodically. It had the minimalist quality of a cappella singing—unembellished, precise, perfect. Not one bell was dissonant.

Athena noticed my distraction, "It is *papou* Kotzu's 'things.'" The Greeks call their animals *things*—a term of reverence, meaning *the things necessary to live.*

Now we heard bells that were closer, also musical but quite distinct. "This is my father. He joins us for dinner." And at that moment, twenty-five sheep barged through the square and froze in the center.

The shepherd, a handsome, white-haired old man in black jodhpurs and waistcoat, coaxed them with his crook, but the *things* were too terrified to move.

Athena shook her head, "He brings the younger sheep with him to accustom them to the village." But faced with the activity of the *plateia,* the woolly teenagers were too terrified to move.

Finally, a black and white dog, barking and snarling, rushed into the square and drove the frightened sheep to a small patch of grass where they settled into their own dinner.

The shepherd greeted his neighbors quietly and joined us.

Here was Michas Tcharikis, *barba* Michas, the man I had come all this way to see, the man who remembered my birth parents.

"*Despinis,*" he bowed magisterially, "it is my pleasure." He pronounced the rehearsed English carefully. Later, he returned to Greek and Athena translated.

To impress him, I used a formal expression, "*Hero poli*" (I rejoice greatly).

"*Hero poli,*" he repeated with pleasure.

He sat with the erect posture of a nobleman joining others of his rank. Yorgos brought the salads and three plates of goat. He gripped the back of Michas's neck and said something like, "You're looking better today, old friend."

Michas pulled out a computer printout from his waistcoat. It was an email in Greek from pomegranate_k. A shepherd with an email account! Electricity had just been introduced here in the 1960s. "Where did you get this?" I asked.

"From the Yahoo." He pointed across the square to a cement block building with a sagging front porch of unfinished planks. On the porch were several barrels labeled KOKINO KRASI and ASPRO KRASI, red and white wine. It was the *magazí*, the general store. In the dusty window was a hand-written sign: INTERNET.

"Tassos keeps two computers," said Athena, "in the back behind the cheese." She picked up a bottle. "Retsina?"

I stayed at the Tcharikis' home, a two-story stone house surrounded by a fence of the same schist.

Before opening the iron gate, Athena paused and opened the tiny glass door of a votive shrine built into the wall. She lit the *liknari* before the tiny icon of Saint George, the patron saint of shepherds. The little clay lamp with its wick floating in olive oil not only honored the saint but signaled to visitors that someone was home.

We crossed a courtyard paved with slate. The silhouettes of two olive trees loomed over us like the protective spirits of the house. The doorway was low and rounded with an arch in the Roman style. The keystone had the date 1723. Athena lifted the latch and the painted wooden door swung inward soundlessly.

"I tell my father to lock," Athena tutted. "But he thinks he is still in the *tselingato*." I tried to remember where I had heard that word, as I followed her through the portal.

The parlor was cozy with built-in bookshelves and inviting furniture. Recesses in the walls held precious mementos—a small icon of Saint Katherine, an amphora from the Archaic period, a Cycladic goddess in all her austere elegance.

But the centerpiece of this miniature museum was in a nook behind the sofa—a life-size manikin in traditional female dress.

As I approached with respectful fascination, I heard Athena behind me, "My mother . . . Father wanted to save her things."

I had never seen any costume similar. Every stitch was made from the flocks, white geometric angles woven into the basic black background. On her head, a black pillbox with a long tassel. And, on her feet, shoes with pom-poms at the toe. In these wild mountains, I expected clothing to be rough and dull, but this was a fluid display of simple, elegant design. It was almost sophisticated.

I had a strange need to thank someone. And when I turned, Barba Michas was behind me. He had driven the sheep to the fold where the dogs patrolled for the night.

"*Efharisto,*" I said to him. Thank you. "*Efharisto, poli.*"

He took my hands and held them oh so gently.

I wanted to ask about my parents, but Michas led me outside. I followed him through a narrow low doorway beneath the house into the cellar. Half of it was stocked with huge amphorae of olive oil, jars of preserves, and wine bottles. "My wife wanted to be sure I had enough," he said.

In the other half was a huge loom, so old it looked medieval. He pointed to it, said something I couldn't understand, patted his chest and thighs, and pointed above. Athena translated, but she didn't need to. His wife had made their clothes on this loom.

I slept that night on a low, wide mattress snug beneath blankets woven from black fleece with white and red angular designs. Athena lit the wood-burning stove in the center of the bedroom to keep the chill off.

For years I had searched, and now I was here, tucked in cozily by these people who were going to give me back my heritage.

My whole existence had been a lie. At my adoption, my birth certificate had been falsified—name, birthplace, parents. They had erased me—Greek, Orthodox, Olympian—and had created a new being to suit my masters—American, Catholic, bloodless. I had always been a stranger in my adoptive home, a misfit in their world.

Then one day, one person risked the wrath of her Catholic superiors and broke the silence. She told me I had a right to know, and she gave me what little information she had, just enough to begin looking. Years later came the Internet and pomegranate_k.

Breakfast was a slice of feta, olives, and gritty coffee.

"Where's your father?"

"He leaves before dawn for the first milking. The mornings are misty and damp in the upper pasture. Take a coat." She smiled at my capote. I felt a little foolish—the American aping Greek tradition.

Halfway up the mountain, I heard the bells. The varied tinkle of dozens of brass bells, so precisely balanced I felt I heard each one individually.

"The bells . . ." I said to Athena.

"Yes, the bells. In Ioannina, I miss them."

The flock came into view. Hundreds of black sheep and white sheep grazed languidly over the rocky, uneven pasture as the morning mist swirled around them. In their midst stood Barba Michas, a statue in his black capote and hood, leaning forward on his crook at an impossible angle.

A ewe and a goat, both solid black, sniffed at my feet.

One of the dogs, barking and snapping, skidded toward me.

"Drogo," Athena scolded. Drogo glared at me but went no further than a growl.

Barba Michas made his way through the herd, patting one here, one there, murmuring soothing words to each.

Slowly and carefully I told him I was honored to join him on his mountain. I hope that's what I said. He placed his hand over his heart and bowed ceremoniously.

I commented on the size of his flock. He smiled proudly—he had about 500 sheep and goats. But he shook his head. Not like the old days. His father had had 5,000 sheep, his grandfather 15,000. "Come. I bring pictures."

Under a large olive tree, he had a small shelter, a pup tent of woven fabric. Out of the tent, he brought a goatskin satchel.

As we settled together onto a smooth boulder, I saw Michas lay his rough hand, oddly delicate in its movements, gently on the clasp before he opened the satchel.

But inside were no photos of my parents.

The first photo was his wedding picture. A fair woman in a flowered headdress stood beside an equally fair Michas, both tall and solemn, clothed in elaborate black-and-white garments, the colors of the sheep from which the wool had come. A necklace of gold coins displayed her father's wealth.

I was growing impatient to hear about my parents but sensed I must be patient; Michas wanted to savor his memories as much as I wanted to gain some. I hoped my indulgence would be rewarded. It was, but not as I had hoped.

The second photo gave me chills. It was again his wife in a black-and-white costume, but behind the handsome woman stood her *village*—beautifully thatched huts like giant beehives, built up with reeds in sturdy overlapping tiers. Smoke curled out of the holes in the top of the domes, and thick herds of goats and sheep, all black, grazed behind the huts.

"Sarakatsani . . ." I whispered.

He nodded, "*Nai, nai.*" Yes, yes. And he grinned that I knew.

Legend tells us that the Sarakatsani, isolated for centuries in the mountains, are descended from the original Dorian Greeks. Like the Vlachs, they summer in the heights and drive their animals south for the winter. Unlike the Vlachs, they have no permanent villages but live in *tselingatos* (temporary villages of thatch tepees).

I leaned forward over his precious memories as he carefully displayed them one by one. A photo of a *tselingato* of twenty or thirty beehives—doors solid, windows and floors covered with neatly woven carpets. His grandmother beside a *tsiatoura*, the temporary shelter used during the semiannual migration, just like Michas's pup tent beside us. His grandfather with the dogs amid thousands of sheep and goats. A teenage Michas leading an elaborately festooned horse.

During all my travels, I had never seen a Sarakatsani in the wild—few people have. Now I sat beside one "in captivity."

Michas was overjoyed with my fervor. From the *tsiatoura* he produced an unlabeled bottle and tumblers. He poured out a clear liquid and added water. We watched it turn cloudy.

"*Tsipouro?*" I guessed, an *eau de vie* distilled from leftovers from the winepress. Since many in this area make their own wine, they also make *tsipouro*, and it is an honor to be offered a man's personal *tsipouro*.

We lifted our glasses.

"*Kalos orisate*" (Welcome), he said. I had arrived.

"*Kalos sas vrika*" (I find you well), I replied. That was the formula—so I had heard. And then, I took another risk. Before drinking I poured a drop onto the rocky ground.

Gravely he did the same.

A libation to the gods. When one lives so close to them, one must always be careful not to make them jealous. He became expansive but I didn't understand. Athena translated, "The Sarakatsani . . ."

I turned round, surprised; I had forgotten her presence, but she had been there, silently watching like a wood nymph. "The Sarakatsani," she translated, "are the aristocrats of the mountains."

Michas placed his hand on his chest, but Athena's voice had a touch of annoyance; she had probably heard this her whole life and was as anxious to be modern as I was to discover tradition.

Was this my heritage—not only to be Greek, but to be the purest of Greeks, like golden Achilles?

Michas and his wife had been part of a tribe that spent their summers on Mount Souli and their winters on the grasslands near Arta.

"It took three weeks to walk from summer pastures to the mountaintops," he reminisced. "Sheep, mules, dogs, chickens. We left the *tselingato* when my wife caught the consumption. I wanted to settle near Arta, but she wouldn't hear of it. 'You can't breathe down there in the *kambas*,' she used to say to me."

"Mother missed the *tselingato* and the nomadic life," Athena told me.

He interrupted, speaking passionately. She listened and then said, "He told her, 'It was too hard on you, mama.' So he bought the house and they settled here in the mountains."

Michas spoke slowly so I could understand the Greek; he wanted me to hear this firsthand. "My wife said, 'It was hard, but it was beautiful.'" His gray-blue eyes had tears. A god who, for love, has accepted mortality.

Athena went on, "My grandmother loved to speak of the old days. She and my grandfather walked to the Rhodope Mountains." The Rhodopes were all the way across the country on the Bulgarian border. That was before the Great War, before the borders were closed in the Balkans. Michas's grandfather had told tales of grazing sheep beneath the land walls of Constantinople itself. But now, Michas lived in a house in Fitea and wintered near the resort town of Parga.

When would he leave for winter quarters?

In a month or so. This is the first time he would make the trip without his wife. He looked away.

Instinctively, I touched his warm hand. He threw off his hood. "It is good you are here. Watch *katsiki*."

We watched a little black goat take a leap that hung for a second over the reclining Drogo then landed behind him with a harmonious clank of her bell.

The next day, I asked Michas if my parents had been shepherds.

"They had a large flock," Michas assured me, "5,000. In the old days, your father would have been a *tselingis,* an arch-*tselingis.*" A *tselingis* is a Sarakatsani leader.

"Were they Sarakatsani?" I asked. This was too much to hope for.

For a moment, he seemed confused, then he said, "Your family—Sarakatsani, one time. But here, they have a house and in Arta a place they rent for the winter."

Where did they live? Mostly, I wanted to know if they had died.

"My father says he will show you where they lived."

He watched me listening to the bells.

"You like the bells," he smiled. "Your mother taught me to make bells."

Athena spoke to her father rather gruffly. I think they were arguing. I think she was saying that *her* mother had taught him the art of belling.

During the next days, *barba* Michas showed me milestones from my parents' lives. We climbed down to Antifitia, the village destroyed by the Communists during the Greek Civil War, to see the stone house where I was born. In the abandoned shell of the house, I walked on the planks of the empty rooms, studied the hammer and sickle painted in red on the broken stone walls, imagined myself living with shepherds, herding sheep.

On the third day, when I climbed to the pasture with Athena, the sheep bleated excitedly, and the same black ewe and goat galloped toward me and brushed against my thigh.

"They recognize you," Michas said.

I felt a sharp pain in the ankle. Drogo had nipped me. He growled halfheartedly then lumbered away. It was just a reminder.

"Aphrodite and Katsiki wait for you," said Michas. "When they hear you, they hurry to edge of the ravine to wait."

I leaned over and studied Aphrodite's face. She was plump and her face was delicate and, yes, quite pretty. Katsiki liked to gallop in spurts around the flock.

Did Michas have a name for every animal?

"He says he does," said Athena.

"But you kill them," I said. "How can you kill them if you name them?"

"He loves them and they love him," Athena replied.

"They trust me to do what is right," said Michas. "It is like giving away your children, but sometimes you must." He pulled back his hood. The morning was warming. We had taken to sitting on the same boulder under the enormous olive tree that hung heavy with fruit.

"Why did my parents send me away?"

He sighed and drifted into meditation. Then he spoke. "When you were born, your parents were so happy."

"Was I the first?"

"Yes, but then, the Andartes take all children to Yugoslavia, even the babies."

Athena stiffened and she watched him curiously.

I was overwhelmed with confusion. I had not been given by Communists to Yugoslavia. "I was given to Catholics in America," I said, adding with some resentment, "My parents never tried to find me."

His voice grew angry. "Yes, we did. *Malista*, of course we did. No one would tell us where our child was."

I felt we were arguing about different subjects. Yes, the Catholic Church, which handled my adoption, refused to reveal my birth parents. Not even to save my life, the office worker at Catholic Charities had told me with righteous pride.

Athena spoke cautiously, like someone calming a man insane with grief. "*Patera*, this child that was taken, what was her name?"

"Ekaterina."

I began to say that my name had been Eleftheria, but Athena put a fingertip over her lips. "Later," she whispered in English. "We will talk later."

Barba Michas walked away from us and waded into the flock, Drogo marching behind him like the loyal lieutenant.

That night, *barba* Michas stayed out in the fields with the sheep. In the house, Athena opened a bottle of hand-crafted wine and told me a story.

"I had an older sister—Ekaterina. She was five when the Andartes took her. It was the *paidomazoma*. You know the *paidomazoma?*"

The "gathering of the children." In 1948, the Communist rebels evacuated 28,000 children from the territories they controlled and sent them to be raised in the Soviet Bloc. Many never returned.

"Your father did not know my parents." My voice cracked with disappointment.

Athena sighed. "My sister, my mother . . . These days you have been here, he felt that they weren't gone." She looked into my face and saw my heart breaking, and she embraced me.

"Many babies have been taken," she offered. "There are scandals. Mothers were told their babies born dead. Lawyers did the paperwork; judges gave the nameless babies their own names. They were put on cargo planes and taken to the United States."

Still I couldn't speak. My chance to be Eleftheria had slipped away.

Athena went on, "Don't be angry with Father. He wanted to give you hope."

"False hope."

She took my hand. "No hope is false. Perhaps some of his story was your story."

The following day, I didn't go up to the pasture until the afternoon. *Barba* Michas and the ewe Aphrodite lay on the ground, back to back, sleeping in the sun. She knew he needed comforting.

Aphrodite heard me coming up the mule path and fidgeted excitedly. Michas ordered her to settle down and go back to sleep. But she struggled to her feet, bleated, and trundled toward me. She nuzzled her head into my hand, leaped over the rocks, and butted my buttocks with her black head. I patted them both, weak with affection and sadness.

Barba Michas rose and limped toward me, his crook across his shoulders cruciform-style.

"I thought Ekaterina would come back."

"I understand."

"I thought she would remember me, look for me." He was pleading.

I always wondered why my parents didn't look for me.

"We looked for Ekaterina. Always."

I, too, had looked for years, for decades.

The sheep were grazing peacefully behind us. The languid sound of hundreds of bells, perfectly harmonized, accented the warm breeze as it rustled the silver olive leaves.

"The bells," he said in English.

"*Koudhouni*," I used the Greek.

"*Zoi*," he added. Life.

In two days I left Fitia. The people turned out in the *plateia* to send me off with gifts—bricks of feta, slices of baklava, loaves of bread, bottles of *tsipouro* and wine.

Tassos gave me his email address.

Yorgos made a speech in Greek, nodding at me periodically. He spoke slowly, certain I understood. I grasped only a few words, but I understood.

Athena and I embraced. Everyone stood in line to embrace me. But Michas wasn't there.

Athena gave me a ring. "My father kept this for Ekaterina. He wants you to have it." I hesitated, but she slipped it on my finger. It fit perfectly.

"The owl," Yorgos said, holding my hand lightly to explain the finely carved signet, "for wisdom. And the olive branch, peace, prosperity."

"We Greeks have a saying," said Athena. "Peace, wisdom, and wealth—these are fragile; they must be protected in the heart."

Athena handed me a handkerchief. But I couldn't bear to use the fine cotton for my tears, so I pocketed it and used a Kleenex from my pack.

"You are too sentimental," she said.

I shrugged. "I am Greek."

I climbed into the car, resigned that *barba* Michas was too embarrassed to come. Or perhaps I had offended him—Greeks are easily offended. But it takes only a gesture to regain their good graces. In this land where Plato discovered the Absolute Ideas, symbols are everything.

As I drove off, I saw Angeliki with her cows. She raised her palm and spoke just loud enough for me to hear, "Remember, brave woman, that you are Greek." I had much to live up to.

Others called out along the road: *Yeia sou! Antio!* Go with the gods!

The gods. These people live with the gods. Their lives are simple, almost austere, but in their faces was no bitterness or servitude, in their souls no hypocrisy. They were always energetic, amused, curious. Life could make them tired but it never used them up.

Adespotos

As I slowly crossed the narrow bridge out of town, I heard the bells.

In fact, *papou* Kotzu was on the other side of the ravine, his sheep distributed in a long, haphazard line along the road. I saluted him and began the long spiral downward.

Around the hairpin were more sheep, lining both sides of the road, dogs militantly patrolling, shepherds in their black capotes dotting the way, nodding as I passed.

On and on went the line.

Ewes, rams, lambs, goats, kids, vigilant dogs. A line of white and black as far as I could see.

The last were Aphrodite and Katsiki. Katsiki leapt to a higher rock—to get a better view? Aphrodite bleated excitedly and set off the others in a frenzy of *bah-bah, bah-bah-bah.*

Drogo turned his back sullenly.

Finally, there was *barba* Michas.

I stopped.

He saluted me, his hand on his heart, his crook planted at his side, erect, like an *Evzoni* at parade rest.

"*Tha thimoume,*" I said. I wanted to say, "I will remember," but I had not quite managed it.

Michas understood; he handed me a sheep bell through the window and said, "*Yia kori mou.*" For my daughter. But *kori* is also a name for Demeter's daughter Persephone, kidnapped by Hades and taken to the underworld.

"*Eisai* Sarakatsani" (You are Sarakatsani), he said.

I put my hand over my heart. *Aristocrats of the mountains.*

Long after I passed the last sheep, the clear air carried the bells to me. They only faded away when I passed the sign, PHOTOGRAPHS ARE PROHIBITED.

But shortly after, I was forced to pause for a goatherd who was leading his flock across the road.

I still hear the bells today.

I have never found my family, but I found my home.

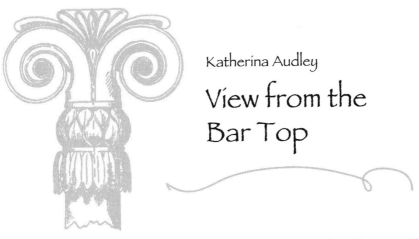

Katherina Audley

View from the Bar Top

"I was not meant to dance on bar tops for a living," I said to myself as I surveyed the cheering drunks below and smashed my glass to the floor. Four months earlier, I had crossed my university's stage and accepted a degree in ancient religion. My thesis focused on the daily religious practices of women in ancient Greece as gleaned through gynecological references in ancient medical texts. Although there was little written by women back then, there were extensive treatises by men on how to treat women's psychological problems (99 percent of which were thought to be rooted in women's reproductive organs), as well as numerous how-to guides on subjects such as training one's wife.

Before continuing on to more advanced studies, I wanted to try learning in a more physical way. "I am going to Greece to learn with my body" was my mantra. Be careful what you ask for. The Fates have a great sense of irony.

I intended to live there through one full agricultural cycle, four seasons, since that was how the ancient Greeks measured time. When I landed on Crete in October 1995, the pomegranates had ripened and split open and were beginning to fall off the trees.

I didn't have enough money to live in Greece for a year without working. The archaeology season had ended, and the olives weren't yet ripe for the picking. So, I interviewed for a job at Time In, a bar where drunken men regularly danced on the black marble countertops. The owner, Tiriago, eyed me up and down during the hiring process and acted as if I had forgotten to wipe something foul smelling off my shoes. He spoke about fifty words of English, enough to hire me, but not enough to really communicate.

"Can you dance?" he asked.

"*Umm*. Sure, I can dance."

"Do you have a dress?" (This said as he disdainfully eyed my outfit: a long flowery skirt, a long-johns shirt, and hiking boots.)

"What kind of a dress?"

"Like, *umm* . . . Cindy Crawford wears."

"No. I don't have that kind of dress."

He gave me 10,000 drachmas (about $50) to buy a dress and shoes, and he told me to come back the next night. The woman in charge of the youth hostel where I was staying pointed me toward a dress shop, where I chose a long black number with a slit up the side and some high heels to go with it.

When I showed up at Time In in my new dress and shoes, everyone stood up and cheered. Tiriago, who looked pleased in his own constipated way, placed me prominently in the center of the bar, and all fifty or so men turned their stools toward me and ordered more drinks.

"Should I do anything?" I asked.

"No, Katherina. *Ola kala.* You are very good. Very, very good."

So I just stood there. One man bought me a drink. I raised my glass to him in a toast. Several others offered to buy me drinks but I had nowhere to put them all, so I politely declined, much to Tiriago's chagrin.

They mostly played a deafening type of Greek music called *skiladika*, which literally means dog music and was the oompah-pah music of the Near East. As the night wore on and everyone got drunk, the music became more and more dramatic. Occasionally someone would rise from his chair, drink in hand, and start swaying, spinning, and stomping in place. His cronies would jump up from their seats, get down on one knee in a circle around him, and clap in time to the music. The dancer would continue to sway, spin, and stomp theatrically, waving outstretched arms in the air, until the climax of the song, when he'd smash his glass down to the floor as his friends cried, *"Opa!"*

Fantastic! I had heard that Greeks sometimes break plates simply to punctuate conversations and was relieved to be living in a place where excessive demonstration of emotion was the norm. Before I left California to move to Greece, my roommate and I had an argument that culminated with my stuffing every dish in our house into my backpack and stomping off to find a concrete wall on which to smash them.

I was eager to join them in their bar-top dancing and plate-smashing fun; but the only dance I knew was the white man's two-step with a shoulder bob thrown in here and there, adding little leaps and claps if the music really spoke to me. Greek dancing came from the hips and belly. Because I couldn't dance very well, my job was to stand behind or on top of the bar and look nice in my dress. I felt ridiculous, but Tiriago was happy because the bar would reliably fill up with customers who would find a stool and turn it toward me as I drank bottle after bottle of Amstel, smoked my Camels, and watched them watching me.

Every night I put on my dress and went to the bar around 10 PM. Invariably, the whole bar rose and cheered upon my arrival. The adulation was marvelous. During the day, as I walked down the street, men who were not sitting with their wives might call out, *"Ela re,* Katherina! *Pama na fama!"* (Hey! Katherina! Come and eat!) I gave them a big flirtatious showgirl's grin and continued to strut along. It was a heady sensation to be treated like a star. I felt powerful, desirable, and in my body.

On weekdays, only men patronized the bar; but on weekends and holidays, women packed in, too, leaving no room to move around. Patrons would climb onto the counter to dance while their party clapped to the beat, sang along, and bought bottles of cheap champagne for the dancer. They'd pop a bottle at the dancer's feet, hand up a sparkling glassful, and the dancer would toast the others below with, "*Stiniyamas!*" (To your health!), take a sip, and smash the glass down to the floor. *Opa!*

During really festive moments, Tiriago would open a family-size pack of napkins and start throwing them around.

"What's up with the napkins?" I asked him, ever in search of a new ritual to study. "Why do you sometimes throw them individually and sometimes in bunches? Is there a specific song that calls for napkin-throwing? Does it only happen on certain holidays?"

Tiriago shrugged and said, "It is fun to throw napkins, here give it a try." He offered me a fistful.

Sometimes, I danced alone on the bar top. Other times, a Greek man would pull me up on the bar to dance with him. My bobbing, lurching dance style must have looked ridiculous in contrast to his sensuous hip swiveling and delicate rhythms, but I got away with it because I was a novelty to the audience, tromping around in my tight dress and long, curly, blond hair. Tiriago would occasionally get my attention and choreograph my dancing with his sign language: He'd put two hands on his one hip, do a little belly-dancer's shimmy, his head cocked to one side with kissy lips.

Attendance started to drop after the first few weeks I worked there. Tiriago bought me a new dress, something short. And red. The numbers went back up. From then on, I was forbidden to wear anything long.

One night, a shepherd came down from the hills with his herd of goats and told me he loved me. One of the bouncers magnanimously translated his declaration of love: "Katherina. You are so beautiful. I am going to give you a goat. Would you like a boy goat or a girl goat?"

I thought it would be fun to have a pet goat. "A girl goat, please."

The next night, he came in with a freshly slaughtered goat and laid her on the counter before me with love in his eyes. He had skinned her body, but not her head or feet, which were still attached. I was still coming out of my vegetarian stage and had not before seen something so recently alive now so freshly dead and about to be eaten. Tiriago and the patrons in the bar were already licking their lips in happy anticipation of the feast. After making certain that my acceptance of his gift would not automatically make me the shepherd's newly betrothed or anything remotely similar, I gave the goat to Tiriago's brother, who roasted her on the spit at his restaurant. We ate delicious goat meat for days.

Despite the hazards of my occupation, the ever-alert anthropologist in me observed and learned rituals such as "making *kamaki*," the Greek man's prerogative to attempt courtship with every female who crosses his path. Making *kamaki* literally means to go underwater-fishing with a spear. When you pass a row of restaurants in Greece, and the waiters call out to come into their restaurant to eat, they are making *kamaki*. If you pass a row of men, and they call out to come and talk to them, they too are making *kamaki*. The fishermen, the waiters, and the players land a small percentage of their targets; but it is a numbers game, so they make a lot of *kamaki*.

Olive season arrived, and the hostel where I lived filled up with migrant workers. I could have easily switched careers at that point and picked olives; but by then I was too entrenched in the drama of my bar girl's life to leave it for something as humdrum as agriculture. A big family from the country of Georgia arrived, as did a band of Polish boys, none of whom spoke a word of English. A young Swedish couple and, a few weeks later, a second Swedish boy also checked in. The Swedish girl broke up with her boyfriend and switched to the other Swedish boy. The Georgian family took over one room and the Polish boys another, while the Swedes and

I spread out through the rest of the place. We lounged around the hostel, made marvelous stone soups, and became backgammon experts.

The Polish boys and Georgian family left for the olive orchards early every morning and returned tired and dirty every night. I went to work at 10 PM and returned at 4 AM. Dogs started barking and roosters started crowing about an hour after I went to bed, and I desperately searched for effective earplug materials.

Tiriago had agreed to pay me for my work, but dodged me every night. He always became deeply and suddenly involved in a crucial business transaction and would irritably wave me away when I approached him, or he would simply disappear. On the nights when it was quiet and he had no immediate distractions, I would ask to be paid. He would say, "*Ah de*, Katherina! There's no one here! I don't have any money to pay you. There is no money here. What do you need money for? You have a nice dress. You can eat at my brother's restaurant when you are hungry. You can have free beer. Here. Have an Amstel. *Stiniyamas.*"

Some of the men, I suspected, knew I didn't really *belong* up there, dancing away. They were my allies, the ones who made sure I always had a lit cigarette in my mouth and a fresh beer by my side. There was a certain level of abuse I was expected to endure, but there was an unspoken line that was rarely crossed. If a patron held me too close during a dance, tried to grab me when I wasn't on the bar top dancing, or treated me disrespectfully, the bouncers or

Tiriago only had to look at the offender to make him back off. The bouncers wondered why I hadn't had sex with either of them, since they were both single. After three months at Time In, many regulars wondered why I hadn't had sex with them either. I heard rumors that I was a lesbian or not actually from America, but from Albania, which explained why I couldn't translate "Hotel California."

The Polish boys acted as though I were a whore. After all, I left the hostel late at night wearing too much makeup, a tight dress, and high heels, and returned tipsy and disheveled every sunrise. They started playing chicken with me when I was in the shower or getting dressed for work. They'd take turns pushing the door open and seeing how close they could get to me before I started yelling. They were big guys—all eight of them—and didn't follow the same unspoken rules as the patrons of Time In. I slept with my Swiss Army knife open under my pillow.

One busy Saturday night, they arrived at Time In. They were a full head taller than most Greeks. I tried to make it to the bouncers before the Polish boys saw me behind the bar. We made eye contact just as I reached a bouncer, who spoke about the same amount of English as Tiriago.

"Those boys. Bad boys. I no want them here."

"Why Katherina? Why they bad boys?"

"They come in my room. They make me *problema*."

That was all it took. Both bouncers did a *Dukes of Hazzard* over the counter and went right for the Polish boys. They fled, but the bouncers caught one boy. I looked away as he was dragged outside; it had already been a rough week at Time In. I was lonelier than I had ever been. Living so far away from anyone who knew me as anything other than the village bar girl was starting to erode my self-esteem. Constant money worries led me to redouble my fruitless efforts to extract cash from Tiriago, even though I knew that eventually he would eject me on to the street when I became too much trouble. More than anything, I was affected by the emotional roller coaster of living and working in a place where at any given moment the patrons were as likely to start weeping profusely because of a sad song as they were to suddenly clamber up onto the bar and start twirling around above our heads. Violent brawls erupted suddenly, subsiding as quickly as they came. Each night began with a freshly swept floor and rows of new drinking glasses. At closing time, I waded through piles of napkins and tinkling shards of broken glass on my way to the door. Lack of sleep and a steady diet of beer and bar nuts made me as emotionally unpredictable as a local. I was determined to get through this night without tears.

A half hour later, Paniotis, the bouncer, came back in and said, "*Ela*, Katherina. We go talk police now." The police station was the last place I wanted to go; I was working illegally in Greece on an expired tourist visa. But I had no choice. We zipped over to the station on his moped and passed through the main station into a back room. The Polish boy was there, all beat up, surrounded by police with black ski masks pulled over their faces and big, shiny knives in their hands. The Polish boy had his pants down. A knife was held to his dick. Terrified, he looked at me, knowing that his fate lay in my hands. This was vendetta in action.

"Katherina! Is this the boy who makes you *problema*?!?"

I knew I would lose Paniotis's protection from that moment on. He was plainly bloodthirsty, and I was about to become the girl who cried wolf.

"No! It is not him! He is good!"

They threw the boy out onto the street. He was banged up but in one piece.

I hadn't known until then that the Cretan concept of vendetta is still practiced. As a member of the Time In crew, I was under Tiriago and his boys' formal protection. To insult me was to insult one of them. It was their familial duty to exact violent revenge on anyone who caused me injury. But after I indicated the Polish boys had *caused me problema*, and then retracted my accusation when they had their chance to do something about it, I became an untrustworthy liar in their eyes. From then on, if someone got gropey, I couldn't count on the bouncers to do so much as look up from their drinks. Shortly after that, a drunk man came in and, banging angrily on the bar, demanded, *"Korepse sto bar! Tora!"* (Get up and dance on the bar! Right now!) When I refused, he threw glasses into the full, sudsy sink where I was washing glasses, cutting my hands and shaking me up.

The Swedes left. So did the Polish boys and the Georgians. It was Christmas, and I was lonelier than I had ever been. I would wake up in the afternoon and stare at the ceiling until nightfall. Women wouldn't talk to me because I was the bar girl, and the men in the village who had already made *kamaki* with me to no avail had lost interest.

Christmas eve was the loneliest night of all. And the busiest. The glass shortage reached critical levels. I was having the pity party of my life that night, bawling over the dishwater and frantically washing glasses in a soaking wet dress. Tiriago was irritated that I was crying, but needed me to keep washing. I ran outside to pull myself together for a few minutes. But I ended up sobbing even more.

Then I gave myself a little pep talk: "Katherina Louise. It is Christmas eve. You are 10,000 miles away from anyone who cares if you live or die. You are lonely and sad. Why don't you give yourself a Christmas present and not wake up alone tomorrow."

I went back in. A boy named Manolis, who had been one of my allies, noticed I'd been crying and assumed I was in unrequited love. With him. He was determined to alleviate my pain. When I got back to my station at the sink, he hand-fed me cigarettes all night because my hands were too wet to maintain a lit cigarette. Twice, he pulled me up onto the counter to dance with him, glass shortage be damned. I liked the way Manolis danced; the way he took my hips in his hands and lined them up with his own and moved us both to the music. I was a better dancer when I danced with him. And he was cute.

Manolis didn't speak English but he understood that I wanted a ride home on the back of his motorcycle. He understood that I wanted him to come upstairs with me. He also understood that it was only proper to sweep me off my feet, carry me into my room like a new bride, and make love to me all night. Afterward, he led me onto the balcony and held me in his arms as we watched the sun rise over the Mediterranean Sea on Christmas morning.

The next day was a bit awkward. It turned out that Manolis spoke even less English than I realized. In fact, he knew exactly two words: *Baby* and *explain*. I thought *explain* was a funny one to know, because even if I tried to explain, he couldn't understand a word I said. He scrunched his slightly simian brow, looked at me earnestly, and said, "Explain." I collapsed in a pile of giggles. His delicate, macho feelings were hurt because he thought I was making fun of him or that he was saying his word wrong. I decided to teach him English, assuming that he wanted to learn. I pranced around the room, like an excited Professor Henry Higgins in *Pygmalion*, holding up objects and speaking slowly and clearly as I named them. He didn't really care about learning English, but he was quite pleased to be the guy who got to bang the bar girl. I didn't mind being a notch on his belt because sex with Manolis was the best I'd ever had.

Like all unmarried Greek boys, Manolis still lived with his mother. He went home every morning to eat breakfast before work so that she wouldn't worry about him. I didn't know what his job was, but his hands were calloused and badly cut, and he treated them with Mercurochrome. Manolis was as uninterested in practicing pantomime as he was in learning English, so I never found out how he earned a living. Once, he snuck me into his room to show me pictures of himself posing with different guns in his military uniform during his mandatory year and a half in the Greek army. But most nights, after work, we drove up to the view overlooking the village and fooled around for a few hours, after which he dropped me off and went home. I felt as if I were in high school, but popular this second time around.

Once I chose Manolis, he became the toast of the town. Men high-fived him, and women thought that he had a magic penis. I didn't realize this back then. I just thought he was a popular guy. On weekends, when local women came to the bar, they surrounded Manolis. He sat there proudly in front of me, smoking his Marlboros and drinking his Famous Grouse whiskey, as the girls glared at me. One night, I looked up and saw Manolis making out with one of the women. The music was loud, and he wouldn't have understood what I said anyway. So I jabbed him in the back, and he turned around from his make-out partner to face me. I pointed to him and then pointed to me and made a cutting motion across my neck. He gave me the famous Greek shrug. I grabbed him by the front of his flannel shirt and slapped him hard, twice. Once across each cheek. He left with the girl.

We dragged out our affair for a few more weeks but the whole village seemed sick of me by then. I was too complicated and foreign. After I chose Manolis, it became disrespectful for other men to buy me drinks and dance with me. Eventually, they stopped coming to see me altogether. I was old news. A cute new foreign girl showed up looking for a job and took my place.

The police suspected I was a prostitute because I wasn't making any money at the bar and was still around. The truth was, I had been living on beer and bar nuts for months. I didn't have any money, but I was too stubborn to go home. One night, the chief of police came in, and Tiriago grabbed me and pushed me fast and hard outside of the bar island to sit with the other patrons, ending my career at Time In.

That would have been a good time to hightail it back to America and get those graduate school applications in. But after four months of dancing on tabletops, I was in my skin at last. Academia seemed unappealing. I'd witnessed weeping Greek men sing and dance passionately through the night to beautiful, old Rebetika songs, as others threw glasses and napkins in the air just for fun. It made me realize there didn't always *need* to be a deeper, hidden subtext behind strange rituals. And when there was an underlying message to be gleaned, it was usually best left unspoken. Sappho wrote, "If you are squeamish, don't prod the beach rubble."

I packed my backpack, leaving half its original contents behind in a heap on the floor, along with all my filthy bar-girl clothes—except for my favorite little red dress. I had heard about a monastery in the mountains where I could stay for free. Or, I knew that I could always follow the migratory path of the foreign bar girls; and knowing the rules better now, maybe I could make a living at it somewhere new. Perhaps there were still some olives left to pick in the south. Lighter now, with fewer expectations, I swung out my thumb and headed west.

Cynthia Greenberg

Vespa '73

Late summer, 1973.

The boat from Brindisi docked at Igoumenitsa, a port on the Ionian Sea that smelled of low tide and bilge. Massimo, in raggedy cutoffs and a madras shirt bleeding sweat, steered our Vespa scooter past shuttered storefronts and cats scavenging through garbage strewn across the sidewalk. I clung to his bony hips as the coast road veered past hillsides terraced with olive and cypress trees. Goats grazed on dry weeds, and oleander split through cracks in collapsing fences of piled rocks.

A man with beefy arms and a Greek sailor's cap waited at a boat launch to ferry us across a narrow channel to the island of

Levkas. Cranking a winch and pulley, he inched his boat along, chain link by chain link, chugging, churning the water with a metallic screech. He took a few Greek coins and some Italian lira for his trouble.

We spent five languid days in a grove of wind-twisted olive trees that cascaded down to a beach. Sea peeked through silvery branches, blue and white rowboats bobbed with the tide. We balanced on slippery stones that jutted above the surface of the water, diving into its ultramarine depths. I read *Siddhartha* aloud on a beach of tide-smoothed rocks, cradling Massimo's head in my lap, his green eyes the color of sea glass peering up at me.

There was nothing much to eat if we didn't catch fish. I picked an olive off a tree and found out the hard way that you can't eat them raw. Watching us catch nothing day after day, a fisherman presented us with an octopus that got tangled in his net. It was chewy as a rubber band and about as tasty.

Our last morning on the island, jellyfish lined the water's edge, undulating in the frothy current, opening and closing like spineless umbrellas, creating a barrier so we couldn't swim. "They're called *medusa* in Italian," Massimo informed me. Storm clouds brewed purple-gray on the horizon.

We boarded a ferry to Patras and arrived late at night in a rainstorm with no lodging available. Wet. Tired. My period started, and all I wanted was a hot bath, a real bed with sheets, and a pillow that wasn't a wadded-up jacket. While I cried, Massimo, always the great improviser, set up the tent and turned it into a sauna with the blue flame of the portable cookstove.

The next morning, with clear skies, we set off toward Athens. Wending our way along the Peloponnese, a wide peninsula with bad roads and rugged scenery, we took a wrong turn.

It was there we met Milos.

I heard the rumble of his Vespa before he zoomed past us like a streak of silver. He slowed to let us pass, then crept up to overtake us again. We roared by him on a straightaway, waving, laughing, until he zipped around us on a dangerous curve, skittering gravel. He zigzagged ahead and behind us in a reckless game of tag, screeching around slow tractors, yapping dogs, and haystacks shaped like flimsy houses waiting to be huffed down by the big bad wolf. Until it started to rain.

With animated hand signals he beckoned us to a restaurant where he ordered skewers of lamb that the waiter brought flaming to the table, chunks of feta cheese so fresh they smelled of sheep and pastures, grape leaves filled with rice and raisins, briny olives floating in oil. And ouzo.

We drank the anise-flavored liquor till the rain subsided and rainbow prisms colored the sky, then he tempted us into the rock-strewn countryside, down dusty roads no wider than goat paths, with promises of fun and more food. "Come," he said in a hearty voice, a heavily accented mishmash of English, German, and

French that reverted to what was probably Greek when the foreign words failed him. "We will *essen und* dancing. *Cirque!*"

At a thatch-roofed taverna we were welcomed like honored guests. The owner embraced us and escorted us to the best table in the place. I was the only woman except for the waitress who shuttled trays of shot glasses and platters of steaming food from the kitchen: moussaka with tangy tomato sauce and gooey cheese, yogurt with garlic and cucumbers, and papery layers of filo dough that oozed honey, cinnamon, and nuts.

"We will now *rauchen*," Milos exclaimed. Although neither of us smoked, to be polite, we puffed our host's home-grown tobacco, so green it popped like a joint with seeds, and slammed back shots of fiery ouzo. Then we joined the rowdy line of dancers. The goat dance, more a drunkard's two-step than a dance. Stomping feet, staggering, we held each other up so we wouldn't fall down to music so bizarre I couldn't quite find the beat, but I couldn't sit still.

We spent the night in the loft above the taverna. Oregano drying in the rafters, aromatic and sweet, scented my dreams when I finally slept. The whirling in my head and the music and stomping still going on below kept me awake. Also, something bothered me about our new friend. I was glad Massimo had positioned himself between Milos and me. I wasn't exactly worried he might molest me in the night—flat on his back, snoring, he seemed pretty harmless—but what if he woke up?

There was something shady about him. It wasn't just his shiny clothes, or the one eye that looked off in a different direction from the other, or the way he cleaned his fingernails with a dagger, or even his maniacal laugh, revealing several missing teeth. What unnerved me about him was that every time Massimo and I said we needed to be on our way, he showed us pictures of young travelers: "Bob *und* Sue from USA, Horst from Deutschland, Anna *und* John from Great Britain!" He'd point to each fresh smiling face and say, "*Mein* friends," as though that alone would make us trust him. It didn't. It made me wonder what happened to them.

I tried to ignore the voice of fear that warned me to get the hell out of there. I should have heeded my father's all-purpose travel advice: "Don't talk to strangers." I knew we should start heading back to Athens—we had crossed over into territory that wasn't even charted on the map—but Milos was so generous and we were having such a good time.

The desire to have an adventure we could share with friends working dead-end jobs back home overrode our common sense. The next morning, hungover and groggy from bad sleep and too much ouzo, we sipped grainy Greek coffee and followed Milos down pockmarked roads without center lines, deeper into the heart of the Peloponnese.

We buzzed past tumbled-down buildings, whitewash turned gray, tentacles of octopus drying on a clothesline, sponges for sale with the smell of sea still on them. Women in black stood in doorways, scarves tied around their heads, listening to us slice up the silence with mosquito-sounding motors.

Milos seemed to know the owner of every bar along every out-of-the-way farm road. We stopped at all of them. Waiters brought us food and drinks. I never saw him pay. I wanted to know what he did for them in return.

At dusk we slowed near a rock canyon boxed in by cliffs and boulders. Bouzouki music boomed into the street over the sound of our Vespa engines before we killed them. The scent of wood smoke and seared flesh hit me first.

We stumbled into a tent encampment, our thighs pulsating from the Vespa's motor over bumpy roads. A whole animal, a goat or a sheep, turned on a spit, spewing grease into a fire pit. Women in paisley shawls danced around a bonfire while the men smoked and clapped and sang off-key. Milos greeted his friends with slaps on the back and three kisses, then turned to us and said, "*Cirque.*"

Layered in dust, hair matted together in windy tangles, I felt drab and colorless amid the swirls of fuchsia, red, violet, and indigo. Dark-haired children with dirty faces stared from the safety of their mothers' skirts. Raucous laughter roared above the music.

We joined the dancing and feasting, but I just went through the motions. I was beyond tired. Then the circus began: A fire-eater breathed plumes of smoke, a man with tattoos swallowed swords, a juggler tossed flaming torches into the air nearly igniting the trees with each toss. Little people and children stacked themselves into a wobbly pyramid, somersaulted off each other's shoulders, and landed on their feet. A man threw knives at a woman bound to a tree with satin ribbons and thankfully didn't hit her. A rubbery contortionist did a yogic dance, writhing beneath filmy scarves. I tried to keep my eyes from slamming shut in utter exhaustion as I watched a woman in a tutu balance on a donkey's back with an open umbrella.

We spent the night in a cave, but I didn't sleep at all, worried that the forest would catch fire with all the kerosene and people smoking. In my paranoid, sleep-starved state I convinced myself that Milos and his friends had killed those young people in the pictures. "What do you think happened to Bob and Anna and Horst?" I'd whispered to Massimo as we'd spit acrid goat meat into our napkins and slipped it to the skinny dogs when nobody was looking. He had sliced his fingers across his throat and stuck out his tongue. Then he'd winked and said, *"Cirque."*

I kept my eyes on the shadows that flickered on the walls of the cave. Firelight, people, and animals coming and going. Night sounds. Hoot owls and badgers, scuffling rats. Dwarves and people who crawled, their shadows like giant spiders, the looming shape of Milos who came to check on us before returning to the bonfire and his friends. I thought I heard our names mixed in their foreign words and menacing laughter and feared that if I fell asleep something bad would happen to us.

At the first light of dawn I prodded Massimo. "Let's go!" He didn't argue. We knew it was rude to leave without saying goodbye, but we also knew Milos would talk us into staying if he knew we were going; so while he drank Greek coffee in a bar, we hopped on our Vespa and raced back the way we'd come, red-lining the tachometer, rocketing airborne over ruts and pot-holes, parched terrain whizzing by, Massimo's hair slashing my cheeks, till we were far, far away.

Winded and rattled, we stopped to pee behind an olean-der bush and heard an eerily familiar vibrato engine. Hearts pounding, we peeked between the leaves and pink flowers to see a three-wheeled truck pulling a wagon filled with hay. We collapsed, laughing with relief.

We only got lost a few times, spiraling up trails that dead-ended at farms, shaded with the mottled light of late afternoon. Miraculously, after hours of doubting we were going the right way, the gas tank with its fuel-efficient mixture of gas and oil hovering near empty, we found the coast route, a refreshing glint of bottle blue and cobalt.

We stopped at a roadside stand where men with gray stubble sat at rickety tables in the shade of a grape arbor clicking worry beads between nicotine-stained fingers. Shaken and parched, we swigged Coke from glass bottles, the carbonation cutting our throats.

In the distance Athens glowed like a beacon.

Consulting *Europe on $5 a Day*, we found a cheap hotel with beds lined up on a rooftop beneath constellations veiled by city lights and diesel fumes. In the communal shower, glorious hot water drizzled over me. Dial soap, piney as a forest, washed away road grime and wood smoke.

We stowed our packs, then set off in search of food.

The full moon rose orange, silhouetting the Acropolis with an amber light. Rows of café tables set on cobblestones, shimmed with matchbooks to balance out the wobble, sat outside souvlaki stands where gyros twirled on a stake. Flaky baklava, cut in diamond wedges, glistened with butter and walnuts.

English voices, the first we'd heard in weeks, murmured around us. We sat at a nearby table and ordered garlicky *tzatziki*, avgolemono soup, vine-ripened tomatoes, and a bottle of Heineken to share. Americans, South Africans, Australians, and Brits exchanged travel stories: where they'd been, where they were going; a cheap place to stay on Crete; a mule ride on Santorini, reputed to be the lost island of Atlantis; windmills scattered on ruined hillsides in Mykonos; on Paros a trail with butterfly trees where monarchs scatter like blossoms in the breeze.

Everyone leaned in to listen when we talked about Milos and the gypsy camp.

"You guys are lucky to be alive," said a bearded South African. "I heard about these people who met a guy in Thailand. He bought them dinner and laced their drinks with drugs. When they got sick, he let them stay at his hotel, and when they died he sold their passports and all their stuff."

I've often wondered what would have happened if we'd stayed on with Milos. He might have killed us, sold us into white slavery, or, at best, inducted us into the circus. I can picture myself rushing into the lion's cage, brandishing a whip and a chair, soaring through the air on a trapeze, or teetering across a tightrope without a net. Or as the knife-thrower's target, cringing as the sharp tip whizzes past my ear to puncture the tree bark.

We left Greece and motored north into the country formerly known as Yugoslavia. In the coastal town of Split we found another idyllic beach. Citrus-scented evenings with saffron sunsets and starry nights. We boiled chamomile flowers and nettles for tea. Snuggled in zipped-together sleeping bags, my head buried in Massimo's thick chestnut curls, I inhaled his scent of saltwater and Dr. Bronner's peppermint soap beneath a canopy of mythology in the sky.

"That's Pleiades, the seven sisters," Massimo said, pointing to a cluster of stars I'd assumed was the little dipper. "And that bright one is Andromeda, the daughter of Cassiopeia, the queen of Ethiopia." He traced a dot-to-dot with his finger, connecting the stars that formed a lazy W. "That's her sitting on her throne. And there's Perseus who slew Medusa and saved Andromeda from the sea monster."

The next day we swished through plastic fly strips into the cool gloom of a grocery store. Two women in drab clothing stood behind a fingerprint-smeared deli case that housed suspicious-looking fuzzy cheese and yogurt a few months beyond its sell-by date. Cans with faded labels collected dust on mostly empty shelves beside Knorr dehydrated soup, shriveled-up grapes, and mealy apples. We longed for the delicious food of Greece.

While we were eating breakfast, a fuel truck overturned on the road, torching the campground where we had just spent the night. Watching the flames consume the colony of tents, ours included, we decided we'd had enough adventure and boarded the first boat back to Italy.

When we arrived, we heard about a cholera outbreak in Naples that would have quarantined us if we'd stayed even one day longer. The papers said the cause was contaminated mussels.

I fingered the Saint Christopher medallion my Aunt Sophie had fastened around my neck the day I left America, and wondered if the patron saint of travelers was watching out for us. We could have died if we'd eaten the mussels from the stand beside the polluted beach where toilets flushed into the Tyrrhenian Sea, or at the hands of gypsies in Greece, or in the fire at the campground in Yugoslavia. Aunt Sophie believed that bad things always happened in threes.

You never know where the road not taken will lead, whether it will be tortuous and fraught with peril, or a gentle slope with beautiful scenery, but it's usually worth taking. At least part way. And maybe a bit of divine intervention helps too.

Amanda Castleman

At the Seashore with Medea

A MARRIAGE UNRAVELS IN ATHENS

The cockroach skittered across my throat. I sprang awake cursing and crying. Then I slapped my bare neck until bruises began to shadow the pale skin.

I knew this would happen if I ate Doritos in bed. In August. In Athens.

But I didn't stop. Pandora's box was empty, devoid even of hope.

My husband had left abruptly a week ago. "I don't want to live together next year," he announced, after waking me with kisses, *tiropita*—cheese pastry, my favorite breakfast—and *ellinikos kafes sketos*. The sugarless Greek coffee was sludgy with grounds: thick like my thoughts, my heart, the very blood in my veins.

"I just have to go," he said.

I stood, drawing on every ounce of haughty grace gleaned in seven European years—the whole arc of our marriage, in fact. "Then go. I'm taking a shower now. I expect to be alone when I'm done."

Silent, I crouched over the fetid drain. All the pipes reek in Athens, even in Kolonaki, the capital's toniest district. This stinking city, built on olives and seawater and the tears of slaves. I trembled with hate, confusing, as always, place and the emotion encountered there.

He slunk out. Paused. Called through the diminishing crack in the doorway, "I'm sorry. I'll love you always. But I have to go."

Sucker punched, dripping, I curled onto the daybed. No one even knew where I was. Last night, we'd returned to a slapdash sublet after months in Turkey, the Aegean, Hungary, and Romania. Every acquaintance had already fled the *meltemi*, the hot winds that scour the Saronic Gulf in summer. Only workaholics and expatriates like us remained, forsaken in this oven of marble and crumbling concrete.

I had 300 euros, a broken cash card, and a broken heart. No clue where I was or who I was anymore. I didn't even know my telephone number.

Yet something bloomed, a subterranean emotion that slid and sloped and eluded scrutiny. Relief? Surely not. Had our marriage grown that foul?

Then I remembered skinny-dipping in Cape Cod kettle ponds, playing piano duets in our damp British cottage, dancing over the cobbles in Rome's Campo dei Fiori, where we fell in love nine years ago. Backgammon on Greek ferries. Flowers in Phoenician ruins. Honey on toast.

I howled. I dug my fingernails into my palms; claw marks shaped like the sickles of Ottoman overlords.

A faint voice fought through the pathos, the Greek chorus of regret and rage: "The stores close at noon on Saturday. Go shopping now or starve all weekend." The reptile brain—that bossy olive-size clump at the skull's base—had finally come into its own. Air, shelter, sustenance: Secure these, then dissolve.

I zombied into the piercing sunshine and back again. Fuelled on despair and bitter coffee dregs and some primitive directive. Don't let the bastards wear you down: *Noli nothis permittere te terere,* to quote the Romans, conquerors of this more ancient land.

"I hope you don't, you know, *do* anything," my husband had said.

An unexpected divorce in a foreign country with no money and no friends? Perfect storm. I scraped for words, then, finally, spat: "*You.* You're not worth suicide."

Greeks are not keen on prepackaged foods. And the stores don't stock fruit—bar an anemic apple or two, some potatoes tentacled like Scylla—since the weekly farmers market supplies the neighborhood. I wasn't about to cook. How could I face the hearth, center of a home, when my heart was suddenly homeless?

So I ate Doritos in bed—defying all common sense in a cockroached land—and swilled *Mythos*, waiting for my family and friends to wake half a world away so I could weep my news.

The next day, I found him at the archaeology library. "Why?" I asked.

He whimpered. I shouted. We cried.

He confessed he'd thrown his wedding ring into the tangled undergrowth on the slope of Lycabettos, the wolf mountain, rising like a canine tooth above the city's cement maw. "If we pull through, we'll get new ones. If not, I want it to rest here."

My husband was wrong, though. Never mind that I'd lost my original band rock-climbing, then had broken my $7-NYC-bus–station replacement, the waves of its Greek meander pattern crashing upon a welded fault line in the silver.

Things cast away lightly can never be retrieved.

I helped him pack. I kissed away his tears. At the end, when he ran into my arms time and time again, I pushed him away. *Go, if you must. But don't dither.*

Strength always was my fatal flaw, the virtue so extreme it becomes a vice.

Being all badass, I went to work.

I didn't get far. Convinced the flat was unlocked, I backtracked through the midmorning swelter. Paranoia teased my neck hairs, a cockroach ghost-army pillaging bare flesh. The universe had upended. I couldn't trust anything.

Starving and spavined, an Odysseus moving ever farther away—not toward—her spouse, I shipwrecked at the *Athens News*. I drafted travel tales about the Ionian Islands, edited articles on the Cyprus conflict, rewrote stories of Greek Assyrians seeking compensation in northern Iraq. When my colleagues seemed distracted, I crept into the toilet and cried, then quickly brewed instant coffee as a cover.

"You drink too much Nescafé," Dino, the news editor, volunteered. "You're thin and jittery." He proffered a smile and a sandwich to soften the criticism. "Eat, *parakalo!*"

Olive pâté—which I loathe—encrusted the baguette, but I obeyed. My appetite was gone, my clothes hung mawkishly on my five-foot-eight frame. The simple acts—chewing, showering, punctuating clumsy English—would slowly sum into a new life, I knew.

I knew, I just didn't care.

But Athens is not a city that will be ignored.

Squint just right and the capitol is postcard-passable: a clutter of whitewashed cupolas against a peacock sea. Look closely: Smog and rust stain the flaking tower blocks. Sewage runs in the potholed streets. It seems like the wave of Western civilization crested and began its slow drag back to the shore, leaving only a scum ring to mark its highest point here.

No, it's not that bad, really. But I feel broken and broken is all I see.

Athens plucks my nerves one by one. The heat, the grime, the dirty old men who hiss and clack their *komboloi*, worry beads. Eurotrashettes lurching on spike heels. Delivery trucks squalling like amplified alley cats. Trance beats pulsing the windowpanes until 3 AM, 4 AM, dawn. The boutique that sells nothing but golden laurels "made with real leaves!"

The endless pre-Olympic procrastination. The shrill bids for respect. The balkanized shreds of the glory that was Greece.

Broken. Useless. Cast aside. The city mirrors the worst I can believe about myself.

I am not the first to scowl at this landscape, its graceful coves surrounded by scorched and shattered earth. The dominant note is harsh: a maiden aunt protecting the wayward heiress.

Henry Miller felt Athens's edge too. "There is something not only arid and desolate . . . but something terrifying too. You feel stripped and plundered, almost annihilated," he wrote in his 1941 classic travelogue, *The Colossus of Maroussi*.

This land gave rise to dark tales, a mythology more lusty and brutal and base than almost any other. The ancient deities behaved like humans—for better and worse—but with *New! Improved!! Superpowers!!!*

Yet it takes wisdom and great strength to accept fallibility. To pass beyond flaws, learning, and still worship the divine, laughing.

I hate Athens as I lie in the studio with flecked wallpaper the color of tobacco spit. I cringe when my coworkers squabble in unintelligible Greek, slamming doors and knocking over pyramids of beer cans for emphasis. Hollow-eyed, I walk carefully amid the traffic and rubble. These streets are mean. If I fall, no one will care—no one with my best interests, that is.

I've never been so alone. Despite the phone calls, the dozen offers of wired money, company, a safe haven, a shoulder to cry on. My mother's passport bulks her lab coat pocket every day in America. If I need her, she won't even pause to pack.

Stubborn, I remain in Greece, amid the isometric angles and haunted hills, soil barely bound to stone, yet dotted with herbs and wildflowers. The fractals, the rugged blooms, they suit my mood.

Athens doesn't let me collapse. I can't sag into condolences and self-pity. This unyielding city forces me to function. And then it eddies and surprises me: Dino offers a sandwich, Dubrovka invites me to Epidaurus, Marigo and I share confidences and cocktails, toasting good reviews of her first poetry volume.

Greece calluses the skin, but softens the soul.

I hide my wounds—not yet scars—best I can. "My husband, *um*, had a . . . family emergency. I need to finish book and newspaper gigs here. We'll meet soon."

Some hope, in fact, lingers. Both sets of parents agree: My older husband is having a midlife crisis. He'll see sense and come home soon. Just hold on. Not that he deserves it, but hold steady nonetheless.

I waver. Could any love remain? Would I ever again trust the man who brought *tiropita* to fuel a heartbreak? Who discarded me among cement and cockroaches?

The Greeks, the wily Greeks, are not easy to fool. After all, they produced the Trojan horse, Herodotus (the Father of Lies), that shifty god Hermes, light-fingered and blarney-tongued. And piercing discourse is a daily event here.

These people adore questions. They initiate personal, probing Platonic dialogues, then launch the corresponding battery of correct answers. What do you earn? How old are you? Shouldn't you have babies already?

Where, oh where, is your husband? Why isn't he taking care of such a beautiful woman?

Why, indeed?

Men suffer for such acts here, at least, in mythology. They lose all they hold dear and wander the earth wailing, often imprisoned in animal form. Cursed, they taint what they touch: bad water in the gene pool, poison trickling down the generations.

Scorned, the sorceress Medea even murdered her children. *That'll* teach him.

I could raze the earth of our marriage, sow salt into the furrows. Gouge his wallet. Besmirch his name. Crack his spirit with a judge's gavel.

But no, I play the alternate ending. The ending Melina Mercouri's heroine suggests in the 1960 archetypal Athenian movie, *Never on Sunday*. The prostitute, Ilya, symbol of impulse over intellect, insists that Medea never hurt anyone.

Every Greek tragedy ends the same for Ilya: the characters—alive and beaming—reunite for a final bow, then "they all go to the seashore."

I stand atop the Acropolis, watching the full moon edge over Mount Hymettus. One night each year, in August, the Greek government opens the most famous archaeological sites. Hundreds slide and jostle on the cliff's marble, worn shiny and slick. We have no extra lights, no barriers, no safety considerations.

We have no accidents either.

Plum shadows outline the Parthenon. This buttress of land, the art upon it—defying time and Turkish detonations—are so ancient. The moon even more so, a bruised apricot. My woes, suspended briefly between the two, have no weight.

I can carry them with me, harboring a crucible of hurt. Or I can unleash them all into the sky. Scatter them like stars. Let some other fool try to knit together constellations from these pinpricks of pain.

My fingers unclench and flower open. Like Ilya, my body—impulse—trumps my intellect.

"Here I am, watching the full, fat moon in Athens. And soon I'll be divorced," I admit at last to myself. The word is no longer a threat or a weapon. It's a simple statement of fact. Even the greatest loves can end. Mine ends here on the Acropolis: no mean finale.

Dubrovka, her boyfriend, and I slither down the hillside and find a taverna with outdoor seats available. *Mezedes*—small dishes—spread across the table, wine pools in the glasses, the strings of lights shine.

People detach from the flowing crowd and pause around us, friends of my friends. Smiling, they shake my hand. A journalist? Working for *The Athens News*? Could you help with this story, that cause?

An olive tree symbolizes Greece, but it shouldn't. Its deep, lone taproot in no way resembles the people's Gordian knot of interconnected tendrils. Already the vines begin to caress my cheek, whisper in my ear, bind me to this place.

Tonight—baptized by moonrise—I am content to belong, however briefly.

The man I once loved is not invited on this trip to the seashore. He is a world away, cocooning himself in fresh cares, without thought of resolving the last.

And really, that's punishment enough.

I pack my few possessions and catch a taxi to the airport. The driver overcharges me.

My ex-husband always quailed in such situations. "Please don't argue," he'd implore me. "I can't bear it. I'd rather be cheated."

But Greece has restored my strength—or some of it, at least. So I complain. The driver delivers an irate, incomprehensible monologue. We both laugh and pass a calculator back and forth, punching numbers until our sums agree. Then I stiff him on the tip, stare him in the eye and smile.

Oh yes, this exoskeleton will carry me along nicely until a spine evolves again.

The cockroach traced my feeble pulse. He stole among my sorrows, gorging on crumbs. He symbolized everything I hated about Athens: the dirt, the chaos, the flinty greed.

Yet he showed me how to harden, how to survive—and how to take the first steps on the sands of Medea's seashore.

Simone Butler

Finding the Goddess in Zeus's Cave

"Cave!" I shout. Karen hangs a hard right onto the narrow dirt road. It's the first English sign we've seen since we hit the fertile countryside of Crete—surely an indicator that the Cave of Zeus is nearby. Known locally as the Dhiktion Andron, the cave was one of the most important sacred sites of Minoan Crete. Allegedly the birthplace of the phallic god Zeus, it was the site of cult worship as early as 2800 BC. According to a spiritual tour guide I had met, merely touching the luminous formations in this cave will change your DNA. I'm not sure what that means, but it sounds empowering and I'm eager to try it.

"How do we know it's the Cave of Zeus?" Karen asks, as we bump along in our rickety green Honda, stirring up dust. "We don't," I reply, "but it's worth a try." A map of Crete has brought us to Avdou, a tranquil little town with modest pink and white houses surrounded by lush gardens. Life in this part of Crete has changed little over the centuries. Grandmas still wear old-fashioned black dresses and embroider delicate white lace tablecloths and bedspreads to sell in local shops.

This is the *real Greece* that had eluded us thus far in our three-week sojourn from Athens down the Cyclades island chain to Mykonos and Santorini. In Athens, we gaped at the ruins of the Parthenon and shopped deliriously at an endless bazaar in the Plaka. Mykonos lived up to its reputation as a hedonistic resort; we sipped piña coladas and swam in the warm, turquoise sea by day and danced all night. Santorini took our breath away with its bougainvillea-covered white buildings against the blue sky, sweeping views of volcanic islands, and handsome young deckhands.

Though we adored those tourist meccas, we're thrilled to finally be drinking the authentic brew. We had stopped for lunch earlier in Kasteli, a town slightly larger than Avdou, where the waitress spoke a smattering of English. After we ate our chicken salads, and fed the local cats the remnants, we strolled down the street into a bar that stood wide open and empty. Siesta time, the heat of the afternoon. Thousands of CDs hung from the ceiling and papered the walls. Here, a shrine to a long-dead musician next to an ancient Victrola. There, a mosaic sculpture made of broken 78s and beer cans. We peered around in awe, then slipped out as quietly as we'd come in. Despite its festive decor, the place was silent as a tomb.

Now the afternoon is wearing on, and we are far from our rooms at the Pennystella Apartments in the seaside town of Hagia Pelagia on Crete's northern coast. The night before, the overbearing but well-meaning proprietor, Nikos, had assured us in his broken English that we'd find the Cave of Zeus in Psichro, a tiny village in the Lasithi district on the western side of Crete. We'd heard rumors that the cave was elsewhere. So we're going on faith, venturing ever farther into the wilderness of unknown gods.

Faith is something I'd been pondering a lot since the illness and death of my mother four months prior to my trip. ALS had paralyzed her throat. First she lost the ability to speak, then to eat. A feeding tube kept her alive for another year. But when she was unable to get out of bed, things went rapidly downhill. It was a terrible end for a glamorous woman who'd fronted big bands and whose greatest joy was singing in the church choir. The ordeal took a lot out of me, and this trip is my attempt to affirm life anew. I also turned fifty two months ago. Perhaps that's why the idea of changing my DNA sounds so appealing— it's the second half of life, time to make a fresh start.

"What's that smell?" asks Karen, interrupting my train of thought. I'd wondered the same thing. It reminds me of manure, with a briny overtone. "Do you see any horses around?" I ask. We'd seen a sign for stables earlier, and I knew that Karen, an avid horsewoman, was pining to ride.

"No," she says, "that's not it. I'd know their scent anywhere." Gazing at the bushy, gray-green olive trees stretching throughout the valley, we realize that it's the pungent aroma of the trees in the sultry September breeze.

It's been a half hour and we haven't seen another sign for the promised cave. We're starting to worry. "Let's pull off over there," I say, pointing to some looming rocks that look as if they might hide a cave. We park next to an old, blue Vespa, whose owner is nowhere in sight, then scramble around in the brush, looking for a path. Karen climbs up a craggy promontory, and I take her picture. It feels good to stretch my legs and get my heart pumping. The air is alive with the songs of sparrows, the heady fragrance of sage, and the sound of bells tinkling in the distance, tied to the goats we'd seen earlier. But after pushing through brambles around granite boulders, we find no cave.

"Let's pick some of this sage before we go," I say, grabbing stalks of the spiky gray herb to make a tea to help my digestion. Suddenly we hear a shout that stops us in our tracks. A pint-size old man rounds the bend, eyeing us fiercely. Rifle in hand, he yells at us in Greek. We are caught, red-handed. Karen starts talking, fast.

"We are from California. Everyone picks sage there all the time. We don't know the customs here. Would you please put that gun down so we can talk?"

Finally, the old man realizes he has scared us half to death. He opens the rifle and empties it of bullets to demonstrate he isn't going to shoot. We breathe a sigh of relief. Nodding and smiling, we repeat the only Greek word we know—"*Ef-ha-ree-STO!* Thank you!" Then we hurry back to the Honda, sage in hand.

"What do you suppose he was hunting?" I ask as we drive away. "I don't know," Karen grins, "but I'm glad it wasn't California girls!" This is what I love about Karen—she always finds the humor in things. Still full of childlike enthusiasm at forty-seven, she takes frequent breaks from her secretarial job to follow her favorite rock bands around the country. Though her nonstop motion sometimes drives me crazy, I'm grateful to have her with me here.

We continue down the dirt road and it eventually dead-ends at an elfin church. It's a simple, rose-beige stucco building with gray stones inset on the sides and a brown, wooden door. Fearful of another encounter at gunpoint, I climb a flight of stairs to a nearby building to make sure we're not trespassing. "Nobody here!" I call to Karen, who is already heading for the church door. Locked, of course. Then we go around the back to peer in a window, but can't see much through the dirty glass.

"Does anybody ever use these churches?" Karen asks, tucking her red curls back into her bandanna. We'd seen others like it throughout the trip, though never quite this small. "Maybe it's a family memorial," I reply. "It feels really special."

"Let's do a ritual," she suggests. Karen and I are ritual buddies. We met at a late-night drum jam at Black's Beach in La Jolla one summer seven years ago. She was dancing around the fire in a spidery black outfit. Fascinated by her boundless energy, I asked if I could photograph her for my astrology calendar. We became fast friends, sharing hikes, wild parties, and extended phone calls, mostly about men. This Greek island trip was born over pad thai noodles at Saffron, a local eatery. We talked of exotic lands we'd always wanted to visit. I mentioned Greece, and we both got goose bumps. In an electrifying moment, we realized we were destined to go there together. Yet it took another five years until the time was right.

We sit behind the little church on a rocky ledge and gaze at the panoramic view of purplish mountains and gently sloping olive groves. It's peaceful here—not another soul in sight. I light some incense I brought for this purpose. The fragrant smoke charges the atmosphere. Suddenly we hear a whinny from across the valley. "It's a mare, I can tell!" whispers Karen, her eyes alight.

Feeling deeply connected to the land, I call on the spirits of its ancient inhabitants and give thanks for the opportunity to commune with them. As I speak the prayers, my voice takes on a deeper resonance, as if emanating from an unknown source. Crete was settled by the Minoans, a goddess-worshipping race who lived here from 2600 to 1150 BC. Divinely inspired by the Great Mother, they celebrated the pleasures of life and the body. An artistic people, the Minoans decorated their buildings with mosaics of dancing dolphins and fantastic flowers. Life was peaceful for thousands of years, until the volcanic eruption of 1647 BC in Santorini wreaked havoc throughout the Cyclades. The Mycenaean invasion not long after that sealed the Minoans' fate.

Mom would have loved this place; it's peaceful, like she was. She didn't travel as much as she would have liked; Dad was a stick-in-the-mud and didn't want her far from his side. It would have done her good to have a break from him, but now it's too late. I invoke her name, Kathryn, and Karen does the same for her mother, who died of cancer fifteen years earlier. I dig around in my bag for a small container of Mom's ashes. We walk, circling the "mama church," as we have begun to call it, because it's so small and cozy. I sprinkle my mother's remains around its foundation. Round and round we go, as if in a trance, until at last we are done. My mother's body has mingled with the brown earth. Now she is part of this place.

We set off on a hike, ambling leisurely down dirt paths as the afternoon sun warms our bare arms. The land is alive with the spirits of those who once lived here. I half expect to see a woman in flowing robes with a water jar on her head round the bend at any moment. Suddenly, I remember my dream from the night before and share it with Karen. Someone had moved my mailbox and I'd forgotten to check it. Days later, I find many letters from Mom addressed to Susie (my given name).

"No wonder you haven't been getting her messages," Karen exclaims. "She's been sending them to your child self!" That explains why I've felt so disconnected from Mom since her death. "Go on ahead," I tell Karen. "I need time alone." A wave of sadness and relief sweeps over me. I spend so much time as a capable, in-charge adult, when underneath, a little child is crying for her mama. Now I realize that my mama has been seeking me, too. Tears flow, and I feel her presence at last. In some alchemical moment of magic and memory, Mama and I are once more connected.

"Simone, here's the papa church!" Karen has found another, bigger church with a bell nearby. We sit in its cool shade. "You know," I muse, "I think we had to find this 'mother land' first and connect with it, before we could find the Cave of Zeus." We agree that discovering this magical place was a serendipitous event, one we never could have planned. We'll tackle the Cave of Zeus tomorrow.

The flow of the day leads us onward to the mare. The sound of her whinnies grows louder as our car approaches. White with dappled spots, she is tethered to an olive tree. No food or water in sight. How long has she been here like this? We pull over and Karen grabs an apple. We stroke the mare's head as she chomps with gusto. Never have we seen a creature more appreciative. We dub her Angel, white goddess of Crete.

On a brisk walk among the gnarled olive trees, we spot a herd of horses roaming free. Returning to the mare, we find a foal trying vainly to suck some nourishment from her depleted teats. "Why is Angel tied up when the others are free?" agonizes Karen. We vow to return the following day to check on her.

Hiking farther into the brush, suddenly I see a perfect goat skull glowing ghostly white in the shadows beneath an olive tree. Karen and I are both thrilled at my find. I will take it home and gild it with gold in homage to Pan, goat-headed god of nature. We invoke the nature spirits of the land and ask permission to take the skull. The resulting sense of peace feels like *Yes.* We bid our farewells to Angel, whose agitated behavior tells us she's hoping for more food. "We'll be back tomorrow with more apples!" Karen promises. The setting sun is casting dusky shadows on the land, and our rental car has only one headlight—a danger in a country where motorcyclists roar by so fast and close that we're left shaking.

We reverse our path down the dusty road. But as we approach the turn that leads back to our apartment, a wild idea seizes us. Why wait for tomorrow to find the Cave of Zeus? We throw caution to the wind and head down the winding, narrow one-way street of Avdou. We creep past trucks, and men playing cards and drinking in a garage, who stare at us with undisguised interest. American girls are a rarity in these parts.

I get out the map again, and the route reveals itself at last. In less than half an hour, we've rounded the steep, mountain curves of the Lasithi plateau and arrived at the small, fifteenth-century village of Psichro. We barely notice its picturesque windmills in our haste to make it to our destination. This time, the signs lead us right. The Cave of Zeus, nestled on the side of a mountain just west of the village, turns out to be a major tourist attraction with a café and several shops selling fabulous-looking textiles and artsy items. But it's 6 PM, and everything is closed. Fueled by Zeus himself, we scramble like mountain goats up the steep, uneven cobblestone steps in the direction of the cave. Panting with exertion, I understand why the locals rent donkeys to those unwilling or unable to make the climb. Twenty minutes later, breathless, we reach the entrance. The gate is locked!

"Well, at least we know it's here," I sigh. "I guess we're destined to come back tomorrow after all."

We rest a moment, then make the precipitous descent in the encroaching darkness, shrouded by tall, leafy trees. As usual, Karen runs ahead. I pray to Zeus for safety as I slip and slide on the mossy stones. Thankfully we arrive intact, and our one headlight guides us safely back to the Pennystella.

"Karena! Simona! You find Cave of Zeus?" inquires the bear-like Nikos, who is grilling steaks on the outdoor barbecue. He embraces us both. I pull away, anxious to get to the room and take a hot bath. "It was closed," replies Karen. "But look at this. Show

Nikos your treasure, Simona," she grins. I shoot her a dark glance and head for the room. Karen always finds time to flirt. Back in Santorini, she told a cute waiter where we were staying, and he and his buddy woke us up at 1:30 AM, pounding on the door. Now, as then, I am too exhausted to deal with it.

The next morning, after a refreshing night's sleep, we make a detour to drop off Angel's promised apples. We find her tied to a different tree, which reassures us that she is cared for. Then we're off to the Cave of Zeus. The sun is blazing brightly, making us sweat, so we ascend more slowly than the night before, stopping to rest a few times on an accommodating rock. Reaching the top, we pay our ten euros and enter the gate. My heart beats faster as I see the narrow, yawning mouth of the cave. A sign informs us there are sixty steps down to the icy palace, and to be careful because they're slippery. The air is deliciously cool and damp. I glimpse an underground pool below, lit by spotlights. The enormous cave is full of sausagelike, green stalagmites and stalactites. They hang from the ceiling and rise up from the dark, muddy floor like wet phalli. It's no wonder this otherworldly cave is dedicated to such a virile god!

Awed by the mystery and silence, we touch the knobby lime-stone formations, absorbing their energy. Karen scales a slippery wall like Spider-woman to embrace one closely. I hear her chant-ing softly to it, as some German tourists look on in amusement. We're beyond caring what anyone thinks.

As I sit next to an impressive stalagmite and lean against it in deep communion, I marvel that this amazing place was only rediscovered in 1880. Excavators found tiny gold double-axes and goddess figurines stuck into the crevices of the formations—ancient offerings to the Mother or remnants of early Minoan burials. I can imagine the awe this cave must have inspired, lit only by torches.

Later, in the café over greasy omelets, we congratulate ourselves for persisting in our quest. Our DNA may or may not be altered, but we've had an unforgettable adventure. We celebrate the sacred in a land where prayer and ritual were once a vital part of life. Searching for a god, we discover the goddess. And find them inextricably linked.

Linda Hefferman

Special Delivery

A week before I left for Greece, George Files pressed an envelope fat with American dollars, photographs, and letters into my hand. "Visit my cousin," he said. "He lives a short distance from Athens. Please give him this." He pointed to the address scrawled on the outside of the envelope. "He doesn't have a phone, so you'll have to write to let him know you're coming." Then he taught me a few words and phrases, sounds imprinted on his childhood brain from his mother and the Greeks he'd grown up around. *Yeia sou, Ti kaneis? Kala. Parakalo. Efharisto. Nai. Ohi.* (Hello. How are you? Good. Please. Thank you. Yes. No.) The words rolled around in my mouth like some delectable but unfamiliar food, tasting of freedom and adventure.

I had been accepted to the American Field Service foreign exchange program months earlier; but my assignment to Greece and the paperwork on my host family had arrived just a few weeks before I was to leave. I couldn't believe my luck. Though I'd been hoping for a Spanish-speaking country (the only language offered in my rural high school), Greece evoked images of crumbling relics of an ancient civilization, mythology, beaches, and quaint villages perched on sun-washed islands.

George Files, the father of one of my high school friends, was the undertaker in my small, rural Northern California hometown, a community of barely three thousand, left behind when gold fever swept the area in the mid-1800s. A first-generation American-born Greek, George possessed a genetic makeup that harkened back to the Mediterranean civilization and generations of skin made smooth, supple, and ever-so-slightly greenish brown by olive oil. Like a Greek Santa, George was round and plump with kind eyes, a button nose, and a rollicking voice that always seemed on the brink of full-belly laughter. You could more easily imagine him passing his days under a generous sun than in the parlor of the silent dead. But I can think of no one more suited to fulfill that role in my town, a place where the death of a loved one brought casseroles and jelly donuts to mourners' doorsteps just as often as fresh-caught trout and home-grown zucchini.

Just graduated and eighteen years old that summer of 1979, I wanted out. Away from the minutiae of small-town life, where a trip to the grocery store for a forgotten item could take an hour, trapped in the produce section by a neighbor's long-winded description of every ministration to her diabetic cat. I felt as if I'd grown up in a petri dish, every movement observed and recorded, from what I did at high school (I had my own father as a math and science teacher) to my meandering around town with my friends in my family's dented 1957 VW Beetle, garishly painted with red and white zebra stripes years earlier by my hippie cousins. That summer, my high school girlfriends were exchanging their boyfriends' letter jackets for diamond rings and misty visions of happily ever after, or partying in the woods in the backs of pickup trucks, drinking canned beer and watching boys hold tobacco-spitting contests. None of that held any appeal for me. The story of my life was about to be written, and I wanted it to contain the *world!* Greece seemed a perfect place to begin.

Descending into Greece that August afternoon, I pressed my face to the plane window and gawked at my adopted country spread out below me, her coastline dotted with islands and the iridescent Mediterranean lapping at her shores. "It's so beautiful,"

I murmured, my heart pounding, mesmerized by the exotic dream unfurling below me. I decided then and there I would love everything about it.

I spent my first night in downtown Athens in a hotel room so hot the sheets stuck to my body. Diesel fumes from the bus hub a block away filtered through the open window, and the constant chorus of honking horns never ceased. I found out later that every self-respecting Greek driver keeps one hand on the horn, regardless of whether his honking has any affect on clearing the way through traffic.

At dinner that first night with the president of AFS Greece and four other new AFS students, I excused myself to go to the restroom. The waiter insisted on showing me the way. He followed me into the bathroom and nudged me up against the wall, puckering his lips and leaning into my face. "Little bit," he said, "one kiss." His white shirt was unbuttoned at the neck and a gold chain snaked its way through black chest hairs. A metal cap glinted in his mouth and his breath was hot and garlicky.

I tried to think of something George Files had taught me that I could use in this situation. The only thing that came to mind was *parakalo* (please). "Stop it," I said, and turned my face away, catching a whiff of the sour sweat that stained the underarms of his shirt. I felt my stomach lurch and wondered if he'd leave me alone if I threw up on him.

"*Ela*, just one kiss," he said, pressing harder against me.

"*Ohi!*" I hissed, glowering, and pushed him hard in the chest with both hands.

"Okay, okay. No problem," he said backing away with his hands in the air. Unwittingly, I had learned my first survival lesson in the land of swarthy machismo: Answer rudeness with louder rudeness. Though the experience startled me, it did little to tarnish the euphoria of being in the same city as the Acropolis, which I'd glimpsed from the taxi that afternoon. I felt invincible, wearing my naiveté like a superhero's unitard. There was nothing I couldn't handle. Greece had chosen *me*. And I was ready to accept her fully and adapt myself to her culture.

Contrary to the ideal host family advertised in the AFS brochures (which would have had teenagers my age, who would love me like their own sister), my new family was a young, upper-middle-class couple with two elementary-age boys living in Halandri, a suburb north of Athens. They'd hosted live-in, English-speaking girls since their first son started talking. I was the fifth warm body to fulfill that role, unpacking my suitcase in a tiny room with a flimsy pocket door off the marble-tiled kitchen, a room I shared with the broom closet and washing machine. I placed George's envelope in my drawer and wondered how I would learn enough Greek to visit his cousin if I was expected to speak English all the time.

On the bus into Athens for my first language lesson I sat next to the window, clutching a map and directions in my hand, trying to follow the route and keep track of the stops. The other passengers stared at me—men with potbellies straining against their shirt buttons; old women dressed all in black with thick stockings and clunky shoes carrying shopping bags made of twine; teenagers in tight jeans, stylish sandals, and white T-shirts; young mothers clutching children whose eyes were giant pools of liquid chocolate. When the bus turned down a smaller street, the lady seated next to me said something and gestured to the paper in my hand, then pointed out the window at the bus shelter. I caught the word *stasis,* which I knew meant bus stop. *"Efharisto, efharisto!"* I said, moving into the crowded aisle to get to the exit.

"Parakalo," she said, twitching her head sideways in a gesture I'd learned was a Greek nod. As I watched the bus pull away, I saw her through the window in the sea of staring faces, a slight smile lifting the corners of her mouth and eyes. Walking the few blocks to my language class at the Hellenic American Union, I attracted more followers than the Pied Piper of Hamelin. Guys in tight pants with unbuttoned shirts and gold chains swooped in close if I dared look at my map. "Where are you going?" "Where you from?" "Can I help you?" "American? English? Deutsch? Svensk?" they asked. I glared at them.

"Leave me alone," I said, loudly. Surprisingly they backed up, then scuttled into side streets like cockroaches in sudden light.

After that day I moved through Athens with a feigned confidence. At five foot eight with strawberry blond hair, I attracted a lot of attention—*psst psst pssts* from the men and stares from the women. But eventually the confidence I exuded on the outside penetrated to my core; I owned the city, venturing with icy hostility into even the most touristy areas like Sindagma Square and Plaka (the old town at the base of the Acropolis), where swarms of guys surrounded every fair-haired female, competing in their *kamaki* (fishing) pickup game.

The city became an escape hatch from the tedious boredom of my home life in the Athens suburbs and endless days in drafty classrooms, where I sat writing letters to my family and friends or conjugating verbs from a copy of *Teach Yourself Modern Greek*. As long as I was home to baby-sit when my host parents wanted to go out and I played with the kids for a while every day, I was free to go wherever I wanted, day or night.

I continued language lessons at the Hellenic American Union on my own, which gave me an excuse to leave school and Halandri twice a week. I'd climb the long paths and steep stairs up Mount Lycabettus with the other AFS girls, where we ordered frothy Nescafé *frappé me gala* and looked down on the Acropolis and the vast city of Athens that sprawled out around it. I discovered the best bakeries for warm *bougatses*, flaky pastries filled with sweet custard dowsed in powdered sugar and cinnamon. When the weather turned cold I bought cheap sweaters and corduroys in the long alleys crammed with clothing stalls near the bus terminus, haggling down the price with my ever-more-confident Greek.

As I meandered through Athens, the traffic noise and press of humanity soothed me, as if washing away the stain of stares, boredom, and humiliation. In Athens I was simply a face in the crowd. I interacted with only those of *my* choosing—a congenial exchange with a shopkeeper or bus passenger, a smile and wink at a child—leaving those strangers with nothing more than a fleeting glimpse on which to base their opinion of me.

By the end of March I had a boyfriend, a sweet boy from my school named Yorgos, who spoke no English. As the oldest son, he came and went as he pleased, and we breezed in and out of his mother's kitchen, often catching her spanakopita fresh from the oven. Short, plain, and aged beyond her years, Yorgos's *mamá* seemed constantly covered in flour from making bread, cookies, and phyllo from scratch. She always washed and dried her hands and tucked a stray hair into her kerchief when I came through the door. Sometimes we'd take Yorgos's sixteen-year-old sister with us when we left, making up a story about going to a movie. As soon as we were out the door, she'd leave us to meet with her friends, thankful to get out of the house with only a little lie.

Other times Yorgos and I would sit in the living room listening to records while his mother brought us homemade almond cookies and sludgy, sweet coffee in tiny cups. I did my best to translate Supertramp songs from *Breakfast in America* into kindergarten Greek, while he interpreted the sultry lyrics of Greek pop and traditional songs. One arm around my shoulder and the other hand punctuating his explanation, he'd gaze at me with his hazel eyes fringed in dark curly lashes any girl would die for and say things like, "Greeks know how to express love, love of our country and our people; *agape,* as well as *erota.*"

With so much practice, my Greek quickly reached a new level of proficiency. But I hadn't yet written to George's cousin, and the fat envelope in my dresser drawer nagged at my conscience.

Since I'd arrived in Greece, people constantly asked me if I knew this or that uncle or cousin in Chicago or Philadelphia or New York City. "*Ohi,*" I answered. I'd rarely been out of California; and, compared to the tiny global real estate that Greece took up on the earth, they couldn't comprehend the vastness of America. But in my drawer lay a link, a connection between a real cousin in America who wanted me to visit his real cousin in Greece. They even had the same name: Yorgos Filis and the anglicized George Files.

Early on a crisp Saturday morning in late April, I stepped off the bus in Yorgos Filis's village—after catching a predawn bus from Athens to Thiva. This was a place where time had slowed down, as if the clocks ran on their own leisurely schedule. As I looked around at the small cluster of white houses that composed this village, a familiar feeling stirred inside me, an uneasiness I couldn't quite identify. I turned as the bus was leaving, suppressing the urge to return to Athens, to the security of my hard-earned anonymity. But the letter to George's cousin with directions to his house stopped me.

This village lacked the charm of the Greek islands, where sun-baked white buildings stand in sharp relief against the blue of the sky and the Mediterranean Sea. This was no quaint town where tourists spend play-money drachmas on postcards and worry beads. It was just a small collection of simple buildings tucked into a nondescript inland valley, where a handful of people eked out a living, birthed their lambs, and buried their dead.

I found the house a few minutes after asking directions from an old man fingering his worry beads at the one taverna on the one street. As I walked away, the proprietor ambled into the street to stare after me. I felt their eyes on my back and knew that many more were peaking from behind shutters and curtains in the houses above the shops.

Word of my arrival preceded me—a strange blond girl wearing pants—and when I approached Yorgos Filis's rough-walled, white cottage, the whole family was standing outside to greet me: a man I assumed to be Yorgos, a girl of about twelve wearing an out-grown flowered dress, a little boy, a tiny, stooped old lady all in black, and a wide middle-aged woman with light coloring and blue eyes wearing an olive green polyester sweater and a half apron over a faded black skirt. *"Kalimera. Ti kanete?"* (Good day. How are you?) Yorgos said, addressing me in the polite plural and holding out his hand. He had the look of a man who made his living with his body. His hands were rough, with dirt ground permanently into the cracks in his skin, and his face under his cap was deeply lined though still youthful. When he smiled, it was with his mouth only, his eyes tired and serious.

"Kala, efharisto. Kalimera sas," I answered. As I shook his hand, I thought of George Files, his hands smooth and clean from latex gloves that protected them from the fluids of his trade. Yorgos's wife grinned broadly and took my hand, shaking it up and down, up and down, like I was an old friend she hadn't seen in twenty years.

"Kourasmeni?" (Tired?) she asked. She reached out to take the bag and sweater draped over my arm. We exchanged a few conversational pleasantries—details about the bus ride, exclamations over the beautiful spring weather, how I'd found their house. Each time I spoke, the girl said something to the old lady in a language I didn't understand.

"Albanian," Yorgos explained. *"Dhen mila Ellinika"* (She doesn't speak Greek). When the conversation dwindled to an awkward pause, I retrieved George Files's letter from my bag and handed it to Yorgos. I felt my body relax, as if I'd just unloaded a burden I'd carried too long, a burden of the distance separating two worlds and two cousins. Now the gap had been bridged between the two Georges—the American-born father of my friend, Nina, and this Greek farmer in whose veins the same blood flowed.

Yorgos opened the envelope and slipped the wad of American dollars discreetly into the pocket of his worn canvas pants. Then he smiled and held up a snapshot of George Files, his wife, Betty, their children, Nina and John, and their dog. His family clustered around him, thumbing through the snapshots and exclaiming about the *"oreo spiti"* (beautiful house), the dog, and remarking on family resemblances. Yorgos's wife said that she'd forgotten what George Files did for a living; and when I looked up the word in my Greek/English dictionary, she laughed and joked that an undertaker was like a farmer—never out of work.

The letter delivered, I started to enjoy myself, drinking in the oxygen-rich country air after so many months of Athens's diesel fumes and city grime. We sat on wooden benches around the long table in their simple dining room, eating slabs of salty feta cheese drizzled in dark green olive oil and oregano, omelets from their chickens' eggs, and thick chunks of fresh baked bread. I recorded the mealtime conversation on my portable tape recorder to take back to George Files. The Albanian grandmother picked up the tape recorder and turned it over and over, baffled that the voices I played back for her were theirs. Yorgos poured over the letters from his cousin, occasionally asking me to read something and smiling at George Files's simple Greek writing.

After the meal I took a short walk around town with the Albanian grandmother and Yorgos's daughter, whose skinny adolescent legs seemed to be rapidly outgrowing her child body. There wasn't much to see: a small church, a cemetery, the school with a blue metal fence around the dirt playground, one small store (shuttered closed for the midday meal), the taverna where I'd asked for directions, a few houses. But everywhere we went, curious villagers scrutinized me, questioned Yorgos's daughter, and introduced themselves. On the way back, the Albanian grandmother clutched the girl's arm and said something, gesturing at me. The girl pulled away and clicked her tongue, Greek for *no*. The grandmother repeated her request and the girl looked at the ground and mumbled that her grandmother wanted to know why I was wearing pants and not a skirt or dress. I blushed, and answered that many young Athenian women wear pants. But I wondered if I'd committed some unknown cultural insult with my choice of clothing.

A little later, standing in front of their cottage surrounded by the iridescence of early spring grass, I watched an untethered goat eat wild chamomile at my feet. "*Oreo katsiki*" (Pretty goat), I said, casting about for something to say. In a village where time seemed to move at a crawl, the trip from grazing animal to steaming meal happened with lightning speed. In what seemed like one surreal instant, a tiny, three-wheeled, white truck arrived, and a short dark man with a blood-stained apron and a wickedly long and sharp knife climbed out, sliced the goat's throat, and hung it from the roof by its hind legs, blood pouring onto the chamomile. In the next instant he deftly slit the abdomen and, thrusting his hand inside the still-pulsating carcass, extracted a fistful of steaming entrails that moments before had been digesting chamomile.

I wondered if I, in admiring the goat, had caused this death since in this world nothing was admired apart from its function and this goat's function was clearly food. Or was I self-centered to think that the desire to please me, a guest bringing word and money from a faraway relative, would warrant the slaughter of the only livestock besides a few chickens this family seemed to own?

There was no time to contemplate this further, as a bigger problem now lay in front of me. Fried goat entrails swimming in succulent, hand-pressed olive oil were staring at me from the table where we'd eaten a substantial meal barely two hours earlier. Hearing that I had to catch my bus back to Athens before the evening meal, Yorgos's wife had quickly prepared this plate especially for me. *"Ela! Fage!"* (Come! Eat!) she said; the rest of the family would eat later. I took a bite, chewed, and tried to swallow, willing my throat to accept what I assumed was a great delicacy. *Open,* I silently commanded.

Uhm-uhm, my throat replied, tight-lipped and stubborn. The harsh whispers of this argument grew so loud inside my head I was sure Yorgos and his family could hear me—or at least guess at my struggle—as all eyes watched me and my plate of entrails. I chewed and chewed and chewed. But my throat wouldn't open.

Our struggle of wills reached a standoff, neither side willing to back down. The whole family stared, waiting for the look of pleasure that was surely expected. I tried to force the lump back against my palette. My throat unleashed its last defense: the gag reflex. It was clear to me now I wasn't going to win this battle. I had to get this rubbery mass out of my mouth some other way. I tried sticking it back in my cheek to dispose of later when no one was looking. But I had taken a large bite in my eagerness to please. I tried working little bits out of the lump with my tongue and sneaking them down with sips of water. The water passed, but not one iota of that meat would make it past my resolute throat.

Finally I excused myself, mumbling inaudibly around the horrid mass in my mouth. I burst into the outhouse, where my now-angry throat propelled the mouthful into a handful of toilet paper. I felt such relief and such shame—relief to finally be rid of the dreadful thing, but ashamed that I had treated their generosity with such obvious revulsion.

When I returned to the table everything was as I had left it— the family watching my every move, the entrails growing cold on the plate, fat solidifying on the individual pieces. I knew now I could never eat it, not even one bite. I kindly explained that I was not really hungry, still full from the generous omelet they had served only hours before. Yorgos's wife commented that the lack of clean country air must affect city people's appetites. "*Nai*," I agreed, it was very smoggy in Athens. Dignity intact—both theirs and mine—thanks to Athens's pollution.

On the bus back to Athens, the countryside rolled by in the failing light of the spring evening. I turned and watched the village disappear. Despite my discomfort over the goat, I carried pictures in my camera, a smudged letter in Yorgos Filis's thick handwriting, and the audiotape I'd recorded during my first meal with his family. These things would close the circle when I returned to *my* village and the American George Files.

As the lights of Athens grew thicker—clusters of people multiplying into the cosmopolitan galaxy of humanity—I felt the confines of the little village and the awkward meal fall away. Back in Athens, I walked through the late-night crowds, wordlessly following my inner compass home through beloved anonymity.

Marilyn McFarlane

Ancient Paths to Peace

The window in our hotel room in Athens's Plaka district framed a fine view of the Acropolis and the imposing white Parthenon, backed by a few benign clouds floating across the periwinkle sky. The scene, minus the scaffolding, was imbedded in dreams all my life. Now, it brought a lump to my throat because I knew my little sister would never see it again.

My sister, Marian, had been a college exchange student in Greece in 1960. She loved everything about Greece, especially the Easter holidays, and always yearned to go back. She and her husband made plans to travel a few times, but got no closer than the annual festival at the local Greek Orthodox church.

"We'll get there," they assured each other. "Sometime soon."

Two months before her sixtieth birthday, Marian died of breast cancer. During that last, wrenchingly painful week, she smiled when I told her through my tears that I would go to Greece for her.

In the forty-five years that had passed between my sister's trip and the day I arrived there for the first time, Greece had gone through many changes. I was confident, though, that the important things—the temples, ruins, countryside—had remained the same. My husband, John, and I would retrace Marian's steps as best we could. And we'd be there during her favorite time, Easter, Pascha, the most important holiday of the year.

Marian's graduation ceremony took place on the steps of the Parthenon, so that was our first stop. We walked the steep path up the 500-foot limestone outcropping and were awed, as millions before us have been, by the magnificence of the 2,500-year-old structures. We weren't allowed to enter the Parthenon, or even stand on the steps as Marian had done long ago, but we walked the same time-worn stones on the hilltop, marveling at the architectural elegance and the sprawling city at our feet. I could imagine her here, five foot two, brunette, cute as a button, and solemn in her graduation gown. The six caryatids, stone maidens supporting the south porch of the Erechtheion temple near the Parthenon, made me think of my sister and me and my four daughters—the girls she considered hers, too, as she had only sons—standing together, tall and sturdy, graceful, and supportive through one of life's toughest ordeals.

Marian would have noticed the same things I did: the red geraniums on every balcony in the Anafiotika neighborhood; the street of butcher shops hung with skinned goats, lambs, and pigs complete with snouts and ears; the purple wisteria that overhung outdoor cafés where we drank sweet, fresh orange juice and were given samples of honey-soaked pastries by a waitress who insisted we weren't eating enough.

On Marian's birthday we visited Delphi, north of Athens, the site of antiquity's most famous oracle. It sprawls across a craggy hillside 2,000 feet above a valley of olive trees. We walked Delphi's Sacred Way in a river of tourists, all of us following in the footsteps of the pilgrims who once came to ask their questions and hear the Oracle's prophecies. The mystery of long-gone spirits and beliefs imbued the ruins—ancient temples, shrines, treasuries—that lay among almond and cypress trees, yellow mustard, and blood-red poppies. I left a flower, a prayer, and a few tears for Marian on a stone at the top of the site. But the days were gone when I might have asked a woman in a trance, probably induced by hallucinogenic fumes or maybe by the local god, why a beloved sister had to die.

As John and I traveled the Peloponnese, heading south on steep winding roads, the gods toyed with us, blasting us with heavy rain and hail, dense fog, and thunderbolts from Zeus's own hand. It was a chilly, off-season weekend; the roads were deserted and the villages shut tight. We lunched in the car on chips and candy as we crawled through the fog to the top of a ridge. Suddenly, as we turned a corner, an enormous, spooky white tent loomed, fluttering and flapping in the wind—our goal, the Temple of Apollo, under wraps.

The temple, built two millennia ago in gratitude to Apollo for saving the people from a plague, was bare bones now and protected by a tarp from the often-freezing weather. Being the only visitors, we ducked under the rattling tarp and walked among the columns, looking for Apollo, the same god who reigned at Delphi.

John and I felt the power of the gods in the whistling and moaning of the wild weather on this isolated hilltop, and we were glad to descend to friendlier territory on the coast and the Mani Peninsula. The Mani, one of several fingers jutting south from the Peloponnese, was not always a friendly place, and even now it's out of the way, with fewer tourists than better-known parts of Greece. Centuries-old towers of stone dot the rugged landscape, tower homes of clans who fought blood feuds and repelled outsiders. The feuds are long gone, but dozens of towers remain and are still being rebuilt or repaired.

We stopped in Kardhamyli, the gateway to the Mani, and fell in love with the quiet, pretty town at the foot of the Mount Taygetus range. We walked stony paths up Viros Gorge, breathing the spicy-sweet scents of wild marjoram, buttercup, and purple vetch. Olive trees sent old gnarled branches over stone walls; goats wandered through the grass, their bells tinkling. I'm pretty sure Marian never got here, as she liked people more than goats and country walks; but if she'd been with us I would have made her come along—older sister's privilege—and she'd have appreciated it. I remembered times we'd traveled together up and down the U.S. West Coast and how her enthusiasm never flagged. She was up for any adventure.

We drove to the world's best-preserved Greek theater, Epidaurus. Visitors always test the perfect acoustics, standing center stage and whispering, "Can you hear me?" while their friends yell from the back row, "Yes." Even more interesting than the theater to me was the *hospital*. Epidaurus is part of a huge compound, the Sanctuary of Asklipios. People who were ill in fourth century BCE came here for medical help, including surgery, and to dream. In specially designated rooms, while the patients slept, Asklipios, the god of healing, sent them cures in their dreams. The sanctuary thrived for centuries. In the museum there's a stone carving of human ears, commissioned by the king of the Alpine Gauls when he was cured of his deafness.

I wandered among the stone rooms and canals and tubs for ritual bathing, past olive trees and patches of grass, and I wondered if cancer was cured here. If my sister had returned to Greece when she was ill, would she have come here and dreamed of a cure, and been healed by it? I wept, and my husband held my hand, soothing me, and said what's past is past.

Our pilgrimage continued as we approached the ruins of Mycenae, the great city of gold back in 1500 BCE. This once-powerful civilization was also the home of the tragic House of Atreus. Murder, hatred, greed, cruelty reigned—this was definitely a dysfunctional family: Atreus kills his brother's children and offers his brother their bodies to eat. And Agamemnon sacrifices his daughter and is then murdered by his wife, Clytemnestra. It sounds like destiny, unavoidable and full of misery.

It was Easter week when we headed for the island of Crete. The pastry shops in Hania, a town on the northern shore, were filled with decorated cakes. Butcher shops were hung with whole, skinned lambs and rabbits complete with heads and fur-covered paws. Kids out of school, balloon sellers, and musicians roamed the streets. My sister, an elementary school teacher, would have made friends with them all.

At Hotel Doma, a former mansion that once housed the British consulate, our dignified, gracious hostess said that since everyone in Greece goes home for Easter, she would make the Doma our home. The soul of hospitality, she guided us to restaurants, provided maps, and made the necessary phone calls when the rental car gave us trouble. Every morning, in a room filled with antiques and nineteenth-century portraits on the walls, she set out a buffet breakfast—fruit, fresh pastries, coffee, and superb thick Greek yogurt with a Turkish topping made from quince preserves, honey, and spices.

Easter morning came, and breakfast was different. Our hostess proudly served us foods she said were typical of the day: turnovers stuffed with cheese and mint, fried honey pastries, and anise-flavored sweet breads, along with the usual rich coffee and yogurt. She urged us to try a lumpy gray liquid made from boiled wheat, almonds, and walnuts—an acquired taste, I decided. Boiled eggs, dyed deep red and stenciled with leaf patterns, nestled in a basket on the table. No pastels or cartoon bunnies on these Easter eggs; they were scarlet as the blood of Christ.

John and I planned to attend mass in one of Hania's churches that day; but we had the time wrong, and when we arrived, the church was deserted. Enormous palm fronds and guttering candles were all that was left. Smoky, aromatic drifts of incense filled the still air.

We went to another church, and another, to no avail. There would be no attending Easter mass. It was all over and time for families to share Easter dinners.

Disappointed, aware of being foreigners, and feeling that I'd somehow let Marian down, we walked the narrow streets. All the shops and cafés were shuttered. In doorways, grills and barbecues were out, and men were jabbing at chunks of savory-smelling, fat-spitting meat. We heard the distant sputter of fireworks. The air was smoky and the whole town redolent with the aromas of rosemary, Cretan thyme, and sizzling lamb.

We stepped into one last church. A few people were still there, kissing gilded paintings of saints. I dropped a coin in the slot and lit a candle in Marian's memory. It was then I fully understood why my remarkable sister was so drawn to this ancient land. She wasn't Greek Orthodox or even Catholic, but she had lived with these people and celebrated their rituals, and, like her, I felt overwhelmed by the power of the place and the faith.

I hadn't been to mass, but I left the church satisfied.

As we crossed the cobblestone courtyard, I noticed a restaurant, one of the few that was open. Greeks and tourists alike sat at tables under umbrellas on the terrace; nearby a young man in jeans and a T-shirt tended a whole lamb on a spit. Cigarette dangling from his mouth, a beer in one hand, and a brush in the other, he basted the meat as it slowly turned and browned. He grinned at us and flashed the fingers of one hand, twice. *"Dheka,"* he said. Ten minutes. He gestured to the last open table.

We sat. Music and laughter spilled from the kitchen. Ten minutes later the man cooking the lamb flashed a huge knife and expertly carved chunks of meat and tossed them on platters. Smiling waiters trotted around the tables delivering the tender lamb and roasted potatoes and glasses of Cretan white wine. Neighbors nodded and smiled and raised their glasses in toasts. *"Kalo* Pascha!"

Americans, Germans, Italians, and Greeks—for a while, we were family, all Greeks, all caught up in the joy of celebration.

In Hania, and across Greece, fireworks crackled far into the night. My sister was with us, and she loved it, every bit.

Sara Woster

Dodge-Ems

When I traveled to Greece at age twenty-one, I liked my hair large and blond, my booze in cans of silver bullet, and my food smothered in American cheese. My friends were similar to me, and none of us spent much time examining anything about our lives or American culture. My exposure to the outside world was limited to occasionally catching the network news or flipping through an outdated *National Geographic* in my doctor's office. My international travel was limited to a free cruise won by my college boyfriend—four days on a slot-machine-filled cruise ship that made quick stops in touristy, Bahamian ports. Aside from cornrows in my hair, I walked away virtually unchanged from the experience.

Years later, I arrived in Greece as part of a group of ten Americans who were studying Byzantine iconography and working on our own art. We landed in Athens and immediately began a crowded itinerary that skimmed every part of the country in search of obscure churches and museums. Shoved into a white minivan, we saw as much of Greece as was humanly possible. We rarely even had time to unpack, staying only a night or two in each place.

Even at that fast pace, I fell in love with the country. Our meals were served outside on long wooden tables covered with plates of *meze:* garlicky yogurt dips, marinated octopus sliced up like carrots, piles of french fries and french bread, gigantic beans in tomato sauce, roasted eggplant dip, fresh slices of feta cheese drizzled in olive oil and oregano flakes. In the mornings we grabbed custard-filled pastries still warm from the oven; and in the late evenings we ate gyro sandwiches stuffed with french fries. In the afternoons, we drank dark, bitter Greek coffee, and in the evenings water bottles filled with tart and sappy retsina.

I tolerated the relentless schedule because I was greedy to soak up every last thing about Greece. We attended mass in Hagia Sofia, where we witnessed women climbing up a hill on their knees in honor of the miracles of the church of the island of Tinos. We scaled the steep mountainside of Meteora to see the hidden iconography of the monasteries. On a ferry to Santorini I watched dolphins swim in our wake. And in the mountains near Sparta I stood where women had thrown their children off cliffs to spare their being captured by the Romans. We stood on the corner of Thebes where Oedipus had his prophesized meeting with his father. We saw the great temples of Delphi, stood in the healing auditorium of Epidaurus, and entered the beehive tombs at Mycenae. We looked into the waters at Halkis where legend has it Aristotle leapt to his death, distraught at not being able to figure out what science of the tides. I raced barefoot on the dirt floor of the original Olympic stadium.

We were treated in a most gracious manner as tourists. But we were not learning much about the people who greeted us with friendly smiles. So, after the few months in a minivan that had begun to smell of unwashed clothes and the clammy wool of our recently purchased Greek sweaters, we were happy to wind up our trip with a six-week residency in the mountains of Kandili on Evia, the long island that runs parallel to the east coast of the mainland. It is shaped like a kidney bean and rugged with mountain ranges. Our group leader had arranged for us to stay at an estate, located in a small village called Prokopi, a pinprick on the map.

Most foreigners have no reason to visit Prokopi. Greeks, usually plump and elderly women clutching worry beads and icons, travel there on bus pilgrimages to stare at the supposedly miraculous bones of Saint John the Russian encased in glass. Part corpse, part tin man, Saint John is covered with a gold face and gold chest, the rest of his figure made up of skeletal remains. After a few days of watching our attempts to connect with the local people, our host revealed that the locals were calling us The Tourists in an unflattering way. They stared at us from their outdoor taverna tables, from the coffee shop tables, and from behind the counter of the bakery. Nobody responded to our desperate attempts to use our horrible, ten-word Greek vocabulary with anything more than a polite nod.

One man would talk to us—he sold us telephone time and ice cream cones from a kiosk. But he was an outcast. His relatives had come from Turkey three hundred years ago, and the town was still holding a grudge.

"Good morning," he would say. "Ice cream?"

Prokopi was an old mountain village populated by women who still made dowries for their daughters. Many of them worked at the estate and a few were willing to speak to us. Sofia, our cook, was a stocky, formidable woman who would walk past me with an axe thrown over her shoulder and return with a headless chicken in her hand. A few hours later that poor bird's corpse would be sitting on my plate, smothered in olive oil, lemon, and oregano.

"You may still find a man," Safoula clucked as she tried to teach me how to make baklava. "You have a nice personality. Maybe you will find a man."

Garifalia, my weaving teacher, managed to fit her impressive girth next to me on my loom so that I could better hear her tell me in her limited English how bad I was at weaving.

"No!" she screamed. "Bad. Bad. Bad."

"She may or may not get married," she shrugged when others asked how my weaving was progressing. "If she learns to cook, maybe."

We thought we could teach the locals about America, and they could teach us about Greece. If we were being honest, we would have admitted that we were surprised they weren't climbing all over themselves to get to know some genuine Americans. I had been taught by all my American history teachers that the Greeks were indebted to America: We saved their asses in World War II. I also believed that the world looked at America enviously, anxious to adopt our customs and our television shows. So why didn't they want to hang out with us? We were from the superpower that brought them *Baywatch*.

The only Prokopians interested in us were the grade school kids who waited outside the gates of our estate, resting on their elbows on the grass and hoping for a glimpse of my friend Katie with her generous breasts as she walked to town. The boys tagged behind the men in our group, asking about American basketball. None of us had the heart to explain that as art students we lacked more mainstream skills like athleticism. But if they wanted basketball, we'd try basketball.

The kids arranged to hold a basketball game at the height of town activity when tavernas and coffee shops were full of people returning from work. The match took place in the court located in the center of Prokopi. The final score was something like 540 to 12, in favor of the home team—made up of kids half our age and a fraction of our height. No language barrier prevented us from reading the disappointment and disgust on the faces of our young opponents, as they watched us miss baskets and double dribble.

"Bad Americans," one little boy shook his head.

"That was awful," my friend Paul said as we walked away, our heads hung in shame as we passed the embarrassed, silent locals who had watched the debacle from the coffee shops across the street.

"I think they did a lot of uncalled fouling," I tried. "That kid with the retainer totally elbowed you."

"They were twelve years old," he said, shaking his head. "Twelve."

"Yes," I comforted him with an arm around the shoulder. "But they were tall for their age."

If we couldn't get the younger generation, we thought we would try to win over people our own age. We dressed up in our best clothes and drank some wine to loosen up. Then we headed to the disco, a nondescript, cinder-block building we often passed on the way to the beach. Its location was surreal—deep in a wooded valley, far from the road. A beekeeper sold honey on one side of it; a large German shepherd guarded a house on the other.

The disco had a large, hand-painted sign: OK DISCO. The inside was slightly more impressive than the outside. It featured a sunken dance floor and enough blinking disco lights that I thought we had just entered the spaceship from *Close Encounters of the Third Kind*. The Greeks were young, good-looking, and very impressive dancers. Their moves, right out of MTV, mimicked the highly choreographed videos of Madonna and Paula Abdul. The boys did fancy boy-band moves, the girls did elaborate routines in which three girls recreated the frieze of the Acropolis. Thunderous applause followed each song.

My friends and I watched, totally intimidated. But after consuming enough liquid courage, we went as a group onto the dance floor. The locals cleared off as if we were transmitting some disease and stood watching us from the sidelines.

It was the era of Nirvana and grunge rock, and we danced as if we were in a mosh pit, jumping up and down, over and over. When the song stopped, we noticed the young Greeks staring at us with expressions of horror. We quickly gathered our things and returned to the estate.

"They don't like us," we conceded.

"We don't blame them," we admitted.

We were disappointing Americans. We were not good at the two things the world most identified as being completely American: basketball and music-video dancing.

I thought of David Sedaris writing about how Americans hate French people because the French don't run around praising Americans and crying out, "We are Number Two!" That was how we felt. We had been raised to find ourselves fascinating, to believe in Manifest Destiny, and to feel certain that we would conquer Greece like we had the western states. Even the French had wanted Euro Disney in the end, for god's sake.

To reach Prokopi, surrounded on all sides by mountains, you traverse roads so twisted that you should sign a living will before beginning the trek. So we were surprised to walk down to the village one morning and find a convoy of flatbed trucks carrying the metal bones of carnival rides. A carnival was being set up in the village square.

"Tonight," the carnies told us, as they tightened bolts with giant wrenches. "Come back tonight."

That night, bright lights draped every tree in the village. Each ride had lines of ticket holders waiting. Wooden kiosks sold cotton candy and gyros. A band played Greek music, and a stocky Ferris wheel offered rides to those who didn't mind that its rotation barely peaked at the tips of the trees.

It looked just like any small-town, American fair, except for one ride—bumper cars. The cars were in primary colors, rubber bumpers skirted the bottom of the cars, and metal arms fed them electrical power from the ceiling. But they weren't called bumper cars. An ornate sign over the ride read DODGE-EMS.

It soon became clear why this ride had a different name. Instead of bumping into one another, the goal of the Greek version was to dodge other cars. On the command from the barker, music started and the cars delicately moved in unison into an oval. We were confused. We had seen more speed and aggression in a Greek church parking lot. When the song finished, the barker picked a winner to receive a free ride. The winner, usually an old woman in head-to-toe black, was the person the barker deemed to be the safest driver.

Finally it was our turn. We ran to the cars. Lowering our seatbelt straps to the sound of bad European disco music, we roared off, banging into each other as hard and as head-on as possible. At first we were timid with the Greeks, then, remembering they didn't like us anyway, we went after them, too. We raced toward them, elbows out, violent grins on our faces.

The barker was silent. The Greeks waiting in the line were silent. The song ended, the cars came to a halt. We walked off laughing, only slightly contrite that some of the older women were so obviously shaken they had to be assisted off the ride.

As we walked to the Olympic Hotel for drinks, a group of young men chased after us, demanding to know why we had behaved that way. We told them that in America the ride is called Bumper Cars and explained how it was played. We apologized, admitting we had gotten carried away.

They shook their heads and returned to the ride. After pizzas and lots of retsina we left the hotel. The fair was still going strong. We walked over to the Dodge-Ems, drawn by the wild yelling of the barker. The line was now five times as long as it had been earlier. We peeked over the shoulders of those waiting in line and saw that the ride was in complete mayhem. Cars attacked other cars, the drivers looking like homicidal maniacs. Women sported wild and untamed hair; old men made offensive gestures; and children spat and swore. A little cherub-faced girl, with a mean-spirited gleam in her eye, was deemed the winner.

"*Amerikanikis!*" A young man who had been upset with us earlier came over now and slapped us on the backs. "Good. Bumper cars! Very good!"

Finally, we had not disappointed them. We had won over the Greeks by being American in a way they could understand: aggressively.

After that carnival night, we gained more access into their world.

Garifalia invited me to her home and served me homemade jellied liquor and amazing anise cookies. She showed me old photo albums of her family and lamented never having married. She read my fortune from the grounds of my Greek coffee and conceded that I was not so bad at weaving that I would not be able to find a man.

We were invited to the Easter service at the Saint John the Russian church. As people lit their individual candles from the one candle intended to represent the spirit of Christ, I found myself squeezing hands with the woman from the bakery.

At the Olympic Hotel we were invited to play snooker with the young men our age, and at the best taverna in town I was brought next door to the butcher shop to pick out my very own lamb to eat.

At Sofoula's home we ate dinner with her son, and the kiosk man introduced us to his daughter. The village children befriended us again, the basketball failure now overshadowed by the new, exciting carnival ride. "Tell us more," they pestered us as we walked home from school with them. "Tell us more about Six Flags. Tell us about Disney World!"

At the end of our six-week stay, we held an art opening and handed out handmade invitations to the people in town. Everyone showed up, dressed for Sunday church. We nervously passed hors d'oeuvres we had prepared in a small attempt to reciprocate all the generosity they had shown us as gracious hosts in their own homes.

The next morning we left for a final week of relaxation on the islands. As we drove through the square, the people looked up and waved goodbye.

The Greeks have an old and wise culture that I had absorbed and learned much from. And maybe the villagers of Prokopi learned from me that sometimes in the safe oval of a Dodge-Ems ride, it can be fun to pick up the pace and bump things around a bit.

Colleen McGuire

Siga Siga

CYCLING IN GREECE

I first touched Greek soil in April 1975, when you could voyage
from Haifa to Iraklion by ship (now defunct), camp in the caves
at Matala (now prohibited), and watch drunken Greeks dance
and smash plates (now passé). After my flirtation with island life,
Greece remained in my memories a mythic place of sensual pleasure. Years later in New York I fell in love with a Greek god. When
he proposed relocating to his homeland, it was an easy decision
to return to that pleasure center of my youth. My move to Greece
was not official until I brought my bicycle over from the States. I
switched gears, as it were, and eventually hauled, one at a time,
three of my four bicycles across the Atlantic.

Greece is not the most logical of European destinations to take up residence by someone who pledges allegiance to the bicycle. Greeks are insanely smitten with motor vehicles. More than a third of its citizens reside in the capital, and all of them seem to covet a car. Inhabited for more than 7,000 years, Athens is a city accustomed to movement. Yet, when Greeks left their rural domains in droves in the latter part of the twentieth century and flooded Athens, paltry provisions were made for mass transport. A bicycle culture never arose in Greece; it is as if the country went straight from the donkey to the car.

I insisted on living in Thissio, a neighborhood at the foot of the Acropolis, in large part because a pedestrian mall now circles the monument's grounds. In this car-free zone I can move effortlessly on the extended stone walkway while marveling at the surrounding archaic ruins. When I venture outside my provincial precinct, I contend with a city locked in perpetual rush-hour mode.

In Manhattan, I gamely wove in and out of traffic, but in Athens cycling is practically a contact sport. Motor vehicles bloat the narrow streets, struggling to occupy alleyways with all the tenacity of a plump matron determined to fit into a size 8 evening gown. Even my svelte Italian-made Colnago often finds no opening to maneuver around the stalled traffic, so tight is the space between car and corridor. Emboldened perhaps by their numbers, Athenian drivers brazenly discount nonmotorized traffic, making the concept of *right-of-way* a non sequitur.

In such a climate, Athenian cyclists are an uncommon breed, be they commuters, leisure riders, or athletes—a strange phenomena, given that Greece is the home of the Olympics. So imagine my surprise when I discovered that in this urban behemoth of some four million residents, my apartment building is on the same block as the headquarters for a group called Friends of the Bicycle. The Friends organize self-contained rides on which everyone carries his or her own gear and camps out.

Fantasies of Greece usually conjure up beach scenes with blinding blue waters, but four-fifths of Greece is mountainous. I was a committed road cyclist until the Friends introduced me to the poignant treasures awaiting a mountain biker in remote terrain. In the Peloponnese mountains near Kalavrita we came upon a village whose prized feature is a hollow tree so huge that it holds a church inside it. I walked through the carved-out door and sighed when I saw an altar and eight chairs in a circle. Religious icons hung from the inside bark, and you could light a candle as you would in any other chapel. I almost genuflected on the spot.

Biking near Mount Parnassus, we stopped to gorge on wild strawberries clinging to a wall of earth. Sparkling from the morning dew and no bigger than a dime, they had a luscious sweetness out of proportion to their size. In the Greek mountains you'll never go thirsty owing to bountiful sources of healthy, pure, cold freshwater springs that make store-bought water taste stale. Like Napa Valley connoisseurs hopping among wineries, the Friends sampled water from every spigot we passed even if we had just filled our water bottles several kilometers back.

To ride with Friends of the Bicycle is to experience *siga siga* in full force. Translated as *slowly,* my sense of the phrase is that it even connotes a disdain for all things fast. On a Friends outing, the goal of getting from point A to the evening's campsite at point B is secondary to indulging in ceaseless distractions en route. We linger for twenty minutes to watch a fellow rider chase and catch a fat garter-type snake with his bare hands. Forty-five minutes are spent poking around a deep cave using our detachable bike lights for illumination. A good one- to two-hour afternoon nap is de rigueur.

Through the Friends I met Yorgos Altyparmakis, an iconoclastic cyclist and consummate bike mechanic whose family has operated a bicycle repair shop for more than forty years. Yorgos is in his sixties, looks forty-five, and has the biking energy of a twenty-year-old. He has a peculiar fondness for cycling maniacal hours, starting early in the morning and pedaling until eleven or midnight with one or two twenty-minute breaks. Few Friends cycle with him when he sets the itinerary, but I regularly ride with Yorgos. As if hypnotized, I somehow keep pace with him.

On my first outing with Yorgos before I knew his style, I grew concerned when we continued to cycle in the *lykofos* (translated as dusk, it literally means *wolf light*). I became alarmed when darkness arrived. Soon enough, however, I recognized that with a full moon and no cars for miles on a navigable dirt road, this outrageous activity was not only doable but wildly fun. Yorgos and most Friends are committed night riders, and I readily joined their ranks. We take note when the moon is full and plan our rides around the *panselinos* (full moon). What better place for lunar gazing than in the land where this practice was cultivated as a science millennia ago by our pagan ancestors?

About six months before the seventeenth annual Spartakiada in October 2005, Yorgos described this bike event to me, and I gasped, "You mean you guys cycle from Athens to Sparta in one day?"

"Yep," he replied in his typical laconic manner.

"That's about two hundred kilometers!"

"Two hundred and fifty-seven."

Gulp. I did a quick math conversion in my head and concluded that to bicycle 150 miles in a day across a succession of mountains, one would have to be super fit or slightly foolhardy. I felt I didn't fall into either category. Nonetheless, Yorgos commenced his campaign for me to register for the ride. "You're out of your mind," were my exact words to him. It sounded preposterous, but I secretly contemplated his suggestion. Yorgos had ample opportunity to assess my cycling abilities, and if he declared me Spartakiada material, how could I doubt the master? I let the thought simmer for several months.

Although I cherish excursions with Yorgos and my Greek friends, I also get itchy to cycle solo. Among a smorgasbord of more than 250 inhabited islands, each one an exceptional honeymoon choice, I have visited some thirty-five Greek islands, more than half by bicycle.

On Lesvos, Greece's third-largest island, I paid homage to the oldest known female poet in history, Sappho, born in Eressos. There is no official plaque to honor her that I know of, but her legacy survives through the tidal influx to nearby Skala Eressos of female tourists, often lesbian, from all parts of the world. Skala Eressos has a sensibility unlike any place in Greece. Here you can find white tourists with dreadlocks, vegan food, women-only hotels, and aromatherapy reflexologists. Underneath the hip facade, however, a traditional Greek community thrives.

I became intimate with many other islands, too, some of them so tiny—like Pserimos with only forty inhabitants—they are unknown even to mainland Greeks. One of my early favorites was Kos, the Dodecanese homeland of Hippocrates, where I biked to thermal waters in the sea, assuredly frequented by the father of medicine. On Páros, after a half-hour climb from the sea, I reached the Valley of the Butterflies, an enchanting little forest where hundreds of tiger moths the shape of arrowheads lie fairly camouflaged in the trees, forcing you to play *Where's Waldo?* Suddenly, they fluttered their wings and a splash of neon orange pinpointed their presence and put a silly smile on my face. Nearby is a monastery with peacocks perched on tree limbs. On Naxos, I was biking along and came upon a thirty-foot, seventh-century-BC male statue, known as *kouros*, lying not far from the road; it had been left unfinished in its marble quarry. I had admired many *kouros* at the National Archaeological Museum in Athens, but to see one in its *raw* state was startling. On Corfu, Kefalonia, and Zakynthos in the Ionian Sea, I cycled to their highest paved points. In August when the figs are ripe, an incomparable delight on any island is to set your bike by the side of the road and gorge on fresh fruit right off the trees. You peel off the pastel green skin to get at the pink meat, which is juicy and delicious and tastes nothing like dried figs.

On Amorgos in the Cyclades, while resting in a village café and being the only patron resplendent in Lycra, a woman began chatting with me, offering that her brother from Athens bikes a lot, too. *Yeah, right,* I thought skeptically; Greek cyclists are as rare as drachmas since the euro took effect.

I interrogated her: "Where does he bike?"

"Everywhere!"

"What kind of bike does he ride?"

"He made his own bike!"

Hmm. There's only one person I know in Athens who builds bicycles. "What's his name?" "Yorgos Altyparmakis!" What a hoot to run into my buddy's sister who lives on the island of Milos and, like me, just happened to be visiting Amorgos. When she told me her brother had cycled from Athens to Sparta, I said to myself, *Yeah, and that crazy Greek wants me to do it, too!*

I am not and never have been an athlete. I do possess a pound of endurance and a dash of discipline. With those minor attributes, I resolved to tackle the Spartakiada.

The Spartakiada is not exactly a race, although those coming in first are recognized with an award and the event is organized under the aegis of the competitively inclined Hellenic Cycling Federation. Male participants must be at least thirty years old, while females must be at least twenty-five. Riders start at 7:00 AM from the Olympic Stadium built in 1896 and must reach the Sparta finish line by 6:30 PM or be disqualified.

It was still dark when I biked over to the starting point, arriving sharply at 6:45 AM. Of 122 participants, I spotted three other females, each about twenty years younger than me, several elderly riders (the oldest was sixty-nine), and—courageously I'd say—a number of overweight guys. We were all riding thoroughbreds, which is to say, expensive bikes.

As this was Greece, we set off at 7:30 AM, a respectable half hour late. The noisy clanging and clacking of 122 riders clicking into their pedals was a cyclist's version of *Gentlemen, start your engines*. Accompanied by a police escort, we thrillingly rode through downtown Athens without having to battle traffic. This segment of the Spartakiada felt like a fantasy for those of us who commute and cycle daily in *carmegeddon* Athens. Another memorable highlight was pedaling across the majestic Corinth Canal.

For the entire ride there was only one official rest stop: an obligatory ten minutes at the eightieth kilometer in ancient Corinth where snacks were distributed. For the first 150 kilometers we were required to ride together as a pack; then you could break away and do the remaining 107 kilometers at your own pace. Since the first 150 KM were practically all flat, I managed to keep up, but when we reached the mountains the guys left me in the dust. I didn't mind; my goal was simply to finish. The route went from sea level to 2,300 feet over a mountain affectionately nicknamed Kolosourtes (Drags your butt), then another 2,600 feet past Tripoli. I coasted the final 25 kilometers downhill to Sparta, finishing the ride in ten hours with no pit stops, except for the required break in Corinth. I was among the last to finish, but, cheerfully, not *the* last.

There was a ceremony that evening in the Sparta town square with awards given to everyone who completed the Spartakiada within the time limits, and I proudly stepped up to the stage to accept mine. A half dozen or so cyclists received a special award for completing ten Spartakiadas. Greeks have a knack for drollery, evident on this occasion by a hilarious award called Most Fertile Cyclist. "How many?" the emcee called out. One biker yelled, "I have three kids"; while another screamed, "I have four." I believe a father of five won out. The fertility award was presented by Sparta's head priest, who looked quintessentially Byzantine in a long black robe, tall oblong headgear, and gray beard stretching to his chest.

Yorgos rode the seventeenth Spartakiada, too; and when we caught up with each other at the end, we exchanged hearty high-fives. I felt indebted to him for intuiting my cycling abilities better than I could. Some guys questioned my presence at this event, doubting my endurance. But in the end they congratulated me for finishing. I gave all credit to Yorgos, facetiously calling him my trainer. In truth, he trained me mentally more than anything by giving me the confidence to overcome my initial intimidation of the Spartakiada and bike 257 kilometers in one miraculous day across the Peloponnese peninsula.

My cycling adventures provide an unconventional lens through which to view the Greek people and culture. They also dramatize my love affair with this sacred land whose illustrious history and stupendous natural beauty humble me. Were it possible to designate an entire country a World Heritage site, I would nominate Greece.

Pamela S. Stamatíou

A UFO in Greece

My girlfriend Beth and I boarded the *Camelia*, the daily ferry-boat that would transport us from Piraeus to our first island stop, Hydra. Across the deck, an old man sat on a wooden stool. He took a tin cup from his bag and raised it to salute me before lowering it to the wind-chapped lips of his ruddy, whiskery face. I watched, mesmerized, and imagined him to be a thousand years old, right out of the ancient Greek stories I had read in school. As I thought, too, of perfectly sculptured men with names like Apollo and Eros, a boy with the head of Hermes, messenger of the gods, came and sat next to me.

I pretended not to notice his chiseled beauty, his cropped black curls, his somber blue eyes. He told me years later, when we shared our conflicting versions of this first meeting with our children, that he knew I was looking at him that day. He could feel the intensity of my inquisitive stare as I inspected his denim overalls, tight and smooth on his solid golden frame, his white leather high-tops, and the clean and crisp T-shirt that covered his thick chest. When my elbow accidentally grazed the soft hairs of his arm, something foreign fluttered in my chest and moved slowly downward. He turned to me and said, "Sorry," with a long *o*. His eyes then were bright and playful, dancing for me against the blue sea, his grin white, bursting through dark tanned skin. I gasped inwardly. What else did he know how to say in my language?

His name was Dimitris.

Beth and I told him about our night before in the Plaka, Athens's nightlife area below the Acropolis, notorious for clubs and getting *picked up*.

"Ahh, so you like *kamaki*," Dimitris said, nodding his head in amused disapproval. The *kamaki* is a three-pronged spear used to catch fish, and a slang term for the sport of catching women. "I hate these places," he declared. I took comfort in his blunt honesty. Maybe Dimitris was different from the other Greek boys we'd met.

By the time Beth and I disembarked on Hydra, the three of us had made plans to meet two days later in Spetses, an island two stops after Hydra. I didn't have much hope of seeing him again as we waved goodbye from the port. "Rooms, rooms," called out the locals hungry for business. Beth and I held up one finger, then followed a young boy scurrying up a narrow stone street into a magical maze of pastel painted houses. Red- and mustard-colored shutters adorned cracking walls splashed with whitewash. We zig-zagged up the hill, avoiding the donkey droppings as we passed tiny terraces, each decorated with an old olive oil tin planted with a pink geranium. Wrinkled faces and curious toothless smiles appeared in doorways greeting us as if we were the first foreign girls ever to visit their island.

By the following evening, Beth and I both had marriage pro-posals, ouzo hangovers, and painful sunburns. We were walking along the harbor with our new local friends, when I felt a tap on my shoulder. I turned to see two boys, both bare-chested in bikini bathing suits.

"It's me, Dhee-mee-tree! From the boat yesterday!" he cried. He introduced us to the other boy, whose name was Adonis. Dim-itris's eyes sparkled and he said, "Don't go to Spetses tomorrow. Come to Ermioni, my village, and I take you to Spetses with my boat." The town clock struck midnight, and I wondered what fai-rytale I was part of.

The next day, Beth and I took the ferry to Ermioni, a penin-sula on the mainland between Hydra and Spetses. Adonis met us, and we followed him along the port to his uncle's hotel, where he told us we should stay and pay up front. He then led us to his uncle's adjoining souvenir shop to spend some drachmas. When we ended up in a café drinking juice we finally asked, "So, where's Dimitris?"

"Oh, he's fixing the boat. We broke down last night on the way home from Hydra," he said. "But, I take you to him now."

We walked to the other side of the peninsula through back alleys and quiet narrow paths. We saw no faces this time. It was past noon, and in the heat of the day, the houses were still and slumbering. We found Dimitris hovered over a small fishing boat, his dark chest hairs glistening with sweat in the intense sun. He looked up, not particularly happy or surprised to see us, serious and intent on his work. He said he'd see us later and passed us on to Babis, a gray-haired man who was hanging about the harbor. Babis spoke perfect English and took us to eat at a taverna.

A few hours later, Beth and I bumped along in the back of a rickety pickup in the black of night with Dimitris, Adonis, two French girls, their dog, and Agas, a local hunchback nicknamed after a Turkish sultan. We headed for the beach, laden with blankets, wine, and fruit. I thought about the thousands of miles that separated me from my home in Southern California, from my over-protective, upper-middle-class world, and yet I felt safe in the dark with these strangers. A full moon rose higher into the sky, and as the male voices next to me broke into native song and serenaded my naive and hungry soul, I realized that I could do whatever I wanted. No one was watching me. We reached the beach, and when I fell into the coolness of the night sea and into the arms of this boy I'd just met, I felt free for the first time in my life.

What force was it that made Dimitris turn up in Hydra that night? What was it that would keep us connected over the next nine years—on our roller-coaster rides through holiday passions and the ensuing realities of cultural conflict?

I spent the next two days in Ermioni—in paradise. Beth and I ate our meals in Dimitris's home where his shy, slight-framed mother cooked grand feasts of rabbit, fresh fish, moussaka, and *tzatziki*. Plate after plate appeared from her tiny kitchen. Dimitris's father laughed just like Dimitris, especially when he stabbed his fork with octopus and waved it in front of our tightly shut mouths. To be polite, Beth and I ignored our distaste for the suction cups, closed our eyes, and opened our mouths wide to let him feed us.

By day, we explored isolated coves, laughing and playing. We would stomp our feet and dance on Dimitris's tiny fishing boat silhouetted by fiery sunsets and rising moons, and fantasize that we were the only foreign girls in Greece ever to have such adventures.

Dimitris, Beth, and I slept on the family's roof terrace, waking up each dawn in the hot sun. His mother would then come to hang the daily wash, and the clothes would drip coolly over our sunburned bodies, lulling us back to lazy sleep.

Four years later, I was enrolled in graduate school in Washington, D.C., three months away from receiving my master's degree in international relations. It was spring break, and my classmates were interviewing for jobs as foreign diplomats and investment bankers. I wanted to save the Third World, but first I wanted to see Dimitris again. When I left Ermioni four years before, we had cried and exchanged addresses. We'd been writing letters to each other ever since. I wrote of life in America, and my hopes and ambitions for a career. Dimitris wrote, "Dear Pamela, I really have been in love with you. Every day I remember you. Your smile, your eyes, your face, your body, all of you. I would like to meet you again very soon but I do not know when . . . First time in my life I feel love to somebody so much. And the some body is you Pamela. Maybe you do not believe this, but it is the truth. I never say lies."

So, I arrived in Greece for two weeks with my shorts and bathing suit, unprepared for the cold and dampness of spring. I wore

Dimitris's parka as we huddled together on motorcycle rides and walks through lush green fields and fruit groves of bright oranges that hung like Christmas ornaments. That's when it occurred to me that I could give it all up and try to make a life in this new world, an entrancing world that I had such difficulty explaining to my parents and friends.

I went back to the States, got my degree, and then Dimitris and I spent the next five years impossibly in love. I moved to Rome to work for the United Nations, and he came to visit me. I moved to New York, and he made his first trip to the United States. And in between my career moves, I spent a summer in Athens learning Greek and seeing Dimitris on the weekends. One Friday, I was filled with desire and excitement as I sat on the stifling hydrofoil lazily anticipating our reunion at the village harbor. The loudspeaker announced our arrival in Ermioni, and I could barely see Dimitris through the salt-smudged window next to my seat. I descended from the hydrofoil and walked to him slowly, shy and demure. He kissed me, one kiss on each cheek, not as I had imagined on my two-hour trip from Piraeus.

He looked down at my knees showing just below the hemline of my Bermuda shorts. "You don't have a skirt you can wear when you come here?" he demanded more than asked.

"But, you should see all those other girls in their bikinis," I blurted out. He didn't care anymore about the others. I was his girl now, and I was staying at his parents' home. I was the girl the neighbors gossiped about, the *kseni*—the foreign girl that shamed his mother because Greek girls didn't stay in their boyfriends' houses.

But, his mother never said no to him. No one said no to Dimitris. I began to feel the letdowns and disappointments that would plague me daily as I let his love govern me. He never explained the rules of the village—why when we walked down the harbor together he would leave a foot of space between us, or why, if I did something wrong, he wouldn't speak to me for days. He worked as a waiter at a local resort; and while he was gone, I would take long walks unaware that I was offending his parents if I wasn't back promptly at 12:30 for the noon meal. I bought peaches and offered them as a gift, not realizing that his family thought I was dissatisfied with the local figs that his father picked for free.

I hated the noon naps in the heat of the day, having to stay inside and silent, as if I were a small child banished to my room. I tried to do all the right things. I even agreed to go for *volta*—the Sunday evening walk—with his mother. She dressed in her finest and led me to a bench overlooking the sea. I started to sit down but she motioned for me to wait. She opened her purse, took out two tissues, and spread them on the bench. She then lifted her skirt to show a white slip she would sit upon so that her skirt wouldn't get dirty. She offered me tissues too, but I was wearing pants. We sat, looking at each other and smiled. I practiced my few Greek phrases—*Yeia sou* and *Ti kaneis?* (Hello and How are you?)

We laughed and pretended to get to know each other. She later asked her son if I owned a skirt.

Ooufo one woman called me. I looked at her blankly as I tried to translate. "Is that a Greek word?" I asked.

"No," she replied, insisting with frustration that she was speaking English. "You know the people who come from the space," she said.

"Oh, UFO?" I asked.

"No!" she wouldn't give up. *"Ooufo! Ooufo!!!"*

I cried angry, stubborn tears that summer and the summers that followed, frustrated with myself for not leaving, for putting up with what I felt was a slow process of losing self-esteem. I was accused often of being wrong and rude. So many times, I wanted to scream and shout and make his relatives and friends go away. But the crying spells never lasted long, because there was always a full moon again—we'd hop on his motorcycle and escape into the night not far from the rules of the village, to our beach where we would swim naked, and I'd feel the freedom again that kept me going back to Ermioni year after year.

I fought for that freedom for years. I fought for Dimitris, even while his love haunted me, invaded my soul, and gave me pleasure higher than the human heart could ever hope to reach. I married Dimitris nine years after we first met. As we walked down the aisle to Handel's "Hallelujah Chorus," I was sure I'd won the battle. But, entwining two cultures, two religions, two countries, two families, and, most difficult of all, two minds, fast became my new career.

My sixteen years of marriage in Greece have given me plenty— two wonderful children of whom I'm proud—a daughter, Irini, dark-haired, green-eyed, and striking, and a son, Stamatis, a replica of his father. Dimitris has taught me to love, to cherish life for its moments, to appreciate those people who appreciate me. I, in turn, have loved his culture's simple honesty, his people's joy of giving, and their unselfish ways of dropping everything in order to help a friend in need.

Many times when I feel frustrated and speechless, I remember back to when I fell in love with Dimitris, the motorcycle rides, pressed up against the warmth of his Greek solidness, my arms trustingly wrapped around him as we leaned into the curves of the ancient roads. I remember sleeping on beaches lit by full moons, swimming naked at midnight, and waking up to the heat of a Mediterranean sun drying my still-damp, salty skin. One thing I am sure of is that the love I found that day many years ago has lasted and triumphed.

If I knew back then what I know now, I might not have remained here on my little peninsula in the middle of this vast nowhere. I might not have seen the dawn's sun explode up out of the sea like a volcano, dripping red and orange lava down the sky. I might not have smelled the lingering pine on a hot, dry night, while the northern *meltemi* winds blew through my window and spread dust from the village onto my body, as I lay sleepless. I might have missed those tiny ports and pebbly sands where wooden chairs and aluminum-top tables dressed in butcher paper would await me with octopus and ouzo.

Nor would I have ever tasted victory in conquering life's challenges for love in this country called Greece.

Linda Lappin

Fish Soup

The fishermen return exultant shortly before noon. The little Cretan village where I have come to spend a summer's repose suddenly comes to life as the small fishing boats putter into the harbor after a night at sea. The men arrive shouting, leap from their boats to the jetty to secure the ropes, moving swiftly with swagger and pride, knowing they are the morning's awaited spectacle. Everyone flocks down to the jetty to inspect the catch. I follow along. One of the men holds up a strange, mottled brown fish to show the crowd and, for the benefit of the foreigners, says in English, "Look, it flies!" He unfolds a prickly, pleated fin that opens up nearly as wide as the wingspan of a bird of prey. It does indeed look as if it could fly. I imagine it flapping its wings underwater, skimming through drifting forests of green, phosphorescent kelp.

Maria, owner and cook of a *kafenio* in the village, is the first one on the jetty. Maria is a dumpy, motherly, homebody sort of woman in her sixties, always clad in black or navy, a kerchief hiding her gray chignon, with beady black eyes like raisins in a bun. Despite her impish appearance, she is a shrewd bargainer and a keen judge of fish. With expert eye, she observes the quivering display of fins and tentacles laid out on a crate for the villagers to choose from. There are octopuses, rays, moray eels, and many other fish I have never seen before. She is quick to seize the fabulous flying fish, for it will make a delicious fish soup, the one dish this village is famous for, which tourists brave the steep mountain roads to taste. Maria and her rival, Nikos, owner of the other *kafenio* in the village, snatch up the best fish. The other villagers and fishermen's wives make do with what is left over, mostly tiny silvery fish that will be fried in batter and crunched whole—heads, tails, and bones. Today there is to be a feast. Maria will cook part of last night's prize catch for lunch at the *kafenio* for all the fishermen, their wives, and their friends, among whom I have generously been included. I have become friends with one of the local women, Cathy, known to the villagers as Sandra, an American woman married to a fisherman.

The fish dispensed, the crowd disperses and the housewives take their purchases down to the water's edge. Squatting on the pebbly shore, they scale and clean the fish right in the sea, bloodying their hands and aprons. Minnows nibble the refuse. I watch as skilled fingers quickly work through a pail of fish. A quick incision is made in the belly, then the guts are ripped out and tossed into the water, or to the gluttonous cats prowling nearby.

And there we are, sitting at the *kafenio*, waiting for the soup two or three hours later, but who keeps track of time here? Clocks have no authority; time is elastic. The cliffs to the east chart the hours of the day. Strangely alive, they change color, move closer or retreat depending on the angle of light. In the early morning, they are a gray, glistening mass until the sun rises high above them. As the day progresses, they seem to come closer, growing more distinct, every crevice and cranny chiseled in stark shadow, like the features of a face coming into focus. At sunset, they blaze magenta only to disappear at night until the moon casts an ashen glimmer upon their indistinct forms. Watching this slow spectacle is one of my preferred pastimes here.

There are only two *kafenia* in this village, set catty-corner to each other at the water's edge: Maria's and Nikos's. The latter is frequented primarily by German tourists and local fishermen, Maria's by everyone else who doesn't fit into those categories, plus a few fishermen.

Maria's *kafenio* is a low building with a large central dining room decorated with posters of Alpine scenes—the height of exoticism in these parts—four or five bedrooms upstairs for guests, and a spacious cement patio out front, furnished with a few warped wooden tables and rusty chairs. A faded sign advertises rooms for rent in German, English, and French. A string of colored lights dangles from the reed roof. Electricity is provided by a noisy generator kept in a shed next door. The kitchen, partially concealed behind a tattered, floral curtain, is a tiny, not-very-hygienic-looking cubicle with no windows and no running water that opens directly onto the patio. How Maria manages to create such delicious meals in such cramped quarters and with such rudimentary equipment is a mystery better left uninvestigated.

The *kafenio* is the life and center of the village. In small villages like this, it functions as restaurant, café, hotel, grocery store, cigarette shop, town hall, and post office. Here you may sit alone, meet your friends, have a drink or a meal, read a book, discuss politics, play backgammon, or wait for someone or something to kindle your attention. Despite the gaiety, gossip, music, or boisterous conversation that prevail at different moments of the day, the *kafenio* is often a place of solitude, of meditative waiting. It is a place to be alone with one's thoughts, or better still, to be alone without one's thoughts. Nothing happens, nothing interrupts the calm routine: a cup of coffee, a sip of raki, the potent local grappa, while you sit looking out at the water thinking of nothing, observing changes in the sea, in the light, and ultimately, in yourself. You may occupy a chair for hours in the morning or evening without ever being asked to leave or to order anything. The *kafenio* is an arena of social exchange, and whoever happens to be part of village society, even if just passing through, is entitled to his or her place there, whether you consume an entire meal or just a glass of water.

All day long and most of the evening, the local men sit sipping coffee, nibbling pumpkin seeds, or just staring out to sea. The older Greek women frequent these gathering places more rarely. They are at home doing the hard work, hoeing and watering the vegetable garden, tending the goats, washing the sheets by hand. But you will find one or two local women in Maria's, sitting quietly alone during the daytime, waiting for the men who have gone out to sea, for the postman who distributes the mail there and collects outgoing letters a few times a week, for the bread van or the knife grinder, or, perhaps, for a ride up the cliff for a rare shopping trip or an errand in the nearby towns of Ierapetra or Sitia, since few here have cars. Although the men in the *kafenio* may sit idly, the women are always busy, crocheting delicate doilies and labyrinths of lace.

Today I am waiting with the women for the fishermen to join us. Their children play on the little beach below the patio. We have drawn our chairs up around a long plank table spread with a gaudy oilcloth, where an assortment of Cretan appetizers has been laid out: pumpkin seeds, roast chickpeas, olives, cubes of watermelon, cucumber, and goat cheese on toothpicks. The fishermen are off somewhere, tying up the boats, putting their gear in order for the next trip out, rinsing their wetsuits and washing their hands under the village tap. Like the others, I sit with a small hand-woven basket containing a spool of white thread in my lap, a crochet hook in my hand, learning to make an edging of lace. Yannis, Maria's teenage son, who waits tables at the *kafenio,* steps out of the kitchen, carrying a bucket. Noticing my handiwork, he sighs and shakes his head, " And now, you too," he says, pointing to the thread, "have caught the Cretan disease! All the women get it!" My companions laugh as he walks out of the *kafenio* and down to the rocky shore.

When the men arrive, unshaven, unshowered, and famished after a night at sea, their wives give them a teasing welcome, asking what took them so long, since everyone is hungry.

We are a curious mix of locals and foreigners. Pantelis, Sandra's husband, is the leader of the group of five fishermen. He is a tall, long-boned, lanky fellow, with a raggedy beard and long, sun-bleached hair, resembling an El Greco Christ with a suntan. He wears a pair of tar-spotted jeans and a T-shirt full of holes. Just yesterday I helped Sandra launder his jeans in a basin of sea water, using special detergent then wringing them out by hand. The other four fishermen, all in their late twenties or early thirties, are dressed in a similar fashion.

Their wives are Canadian, American, German, and Greek, and their flock of blond children speak a Tower of Babel of languages. The young fishermen are accompanied by an older man in his seventies whom everyone respectfully calls Captain, the rank denoted by the battered marine officer's cap he always wears. When he takes his place at the head of the table, the feast officially begins.

It begins, to my chagrin, with live sea urchins, which Yannis brings to the table in a red plastic bucket. So that's what he was doing down by the rocks, prying off sea urchins for our lunch. He goes back to the kitchen and returns with a plate of lemon slices.

Pantelis frowns at the lemon and demands to know why Yannis has brought it. "For the ladies," he explains. "They like it with lemon."

"Impossible. Lemon is okay for other fish, but it ruins the taste of sea urchins."

Now Pantelis turns to me. "You ever eat these?"

I shake my head. I neglect to say that I am squeamish about raw fish of any sort, with or without lemon.

Pantelis plucks an urchin from the bucket, slits it open with a knife, and plops it on my plate.

"Only here can you eat such thing. In Italy where you live, the sea is polluted. But here it is clean, it is safe."

I look at the urchin. A slimy, grayish pink gelatin quivers in the cup of its spiny shell and oozes over the sides.

"Taste. You must try it." He lifts the plate and nods his head, encouraging me to take and eat.

I can't think of anything less appetizing, but how can I say no? Never refuse a Greek's hospitality, I have been repeatedly warned. I take a spoon, scoop up a bit, and nearly gag as I swallow the stuff. The others laugh at my expression as I am unable to hide my reaction. The Captain calls out for some raki, and a thimbleful is promptly brought to me. "That'll kill the taste if you don't care for it," Sandra advises. I swallow a sip of liquid fire. She is right. It takes away the fishy taste, but my tongue and lips are momentarily numbed.

"Have another?" says Pantelis with a devilish smile, eyes glinting, reaching into the bucket for another urchin.

"No thanks. One is enough." And everyone laughs again.

When the urchins are finished, the next course arrives: a large fried octopus, suction cups and all. Pantelis carves the octopus and passes down the servings. I get a slice of head and a piece of tentacle. As we eat the octopus, he tells us how he caught it: attracting it to the surface with a powerful light then plunging a knife into its head. He mimes the fluid gestures of the tentacles in the water, then the writhing of the death throes. Next comes the battering and knocking to make the flesh tender. Despite this dramatic and somewhat gruesome tale, the octopus is surprisingly delicious.

One fish tale leads to another, especially because it seems to be taking a long time for Maria to make the fish soup. The conversation churns away in an excited tone, mixing Greek, English, German, pauses of interpretation, delayed laughter, puzzled silences. Stories of fish and the sea intertwine with unusual topics about which everyone seems anxious to voice an opinion, such as beach nudity or gay marriage. Very different points of view are expressed in no uncertain terms, as far-flung worlds and cultures collide.

One topic about which little debate is allowed is fish. When it becomes known that I was once a vegetarian, excluding even fish from my diet, a heated argument ensues. This is something the old Captain cannot fathom. The sea is so full of wonderful fish. How can you not eat it, when other people are starving? It's a philosophy, someone suggests; and this seems to make it more acceptable, to confer a dignity otherwise lacking. Ahh, he says, a philosophy, I see. On Crete, it seems, adherence to a creed for the sake of philosophy still offers valid justifications for one's behavior, no matter how anomalous.

Fortunately we are saved from further conflict by the arrival of the soup, brought to the table in an enormous, battered, blackened aluminum pot. Pandelis lifts the lid, peers in, feigning diffidence, sniffs loudly, and then lets out a theatrical grunt of appreciation as a lemony aroma is suddenly unleashed into the air. Ceremoniously he ladles out the soup: large pieces of white-fleshed fish and chunks of potatoes swimming in a clear lemon-scented broth. As the Captain cuts thick slabs of bread for everyone, the table wobbles.

We eat in silence, with gusto. When there is not a morsel of fish or a drop of broth left, the recipe is discussed. Although the ingredients are few and the procedure simple, everyone present claims to possess the one secret, unknown to anyone else, that imparts the special flavor to the soup.

You start with the olive oil. The olive oil they use here is produced locally, from the dusty groves you see on the arid hillside. Nearly everyone has a few trees of their own up there. In autumn the olives are picked by hand and cold-pressed, yielding an oil deep green in color, full of sediment, rich, piquant, and tangy. A drop of this unfiltered oil on a piece of fresh bread is a meal in itself. Pour some of this oil into a pot, be generous but not prodigal. The taste of the soup will depend on the oil, as there are no other flavorings but lemon and onion.

No, someone else claims, the taste of the soup depends on the pot: It must be an aluminum pot, better if old and scraped with a few dents in it. Sauté an onion until it is soft and translucent, but not brown or burned. I try to get more specific instructions about the onion: red, yellow, or white? What about a leek or a scallion? An onion, I am admonished, any onion you've got! The secret is not the onion but the flame, not too high, not too low, even better when cooked on coals. Add the potatoes one per person or more if you are hungry, a teacup of water per person, cover and cook the potatoes over very low heat. When the potatoes are nearly cooked, add the fish. Simmer just a few minutes more until the fish is done, not a second longer. Have the juice of one lemon ready, and add it to the pot just before serving, but the lemon juice must not boil or overheat. What fish? I venture. It doesn't matter, I am told. How can it not matter, I wonder. Surely the flavor depends greatly on the fish? No, no, one of the fishermen explains, it depends utterly on the precision of your procedure. Whatever you've caught will just have to do. You can make it with any fish. Even without fish, someone adds. Without potatoes or onion, adds another. With just water and salt, says Pantelis, and everyone laughs.

After the soup, come fried eggplant and *tzatziki*, then wedges of deep red watermelon, ice cream for the children, and lastly those bitter, unfiltered Greek cigarettes that fill the air with a dense, acrid, blue smoke. The gaiety turns to torpor. The local wine, genuine but overly sweet, has gone to everyone's head in the heat. Just when it seems that luncheon is over and there's nothing left to do but go home and sleep, Sandra rises from the table, saying she has prepared a special treat for us. She disappears inside the tiny kitchen and returns with a large plastic bowl. She places it in the center of the table, then peels off the Saran Wrap cover. "Chocolate mousse," she announces, and the children, playing with toy cars on the cement floor in a corner, squeal with delight and run back to the table.

She doles out a few spoonfuls for everyone. The superb-quality chocolate, flavored with Cointreau and coffee, gives off a strong, rich odor in the heat. The chocolate and Cointreau have been brought from France and carefully preserved for a special occasion. The egg whites have been whipped to peaks by hand, the whole thing refrigerated several hours in the only fridge in the village. It is a culinary masterpiece.

We greedily taste this exotic desert, while Pandelis looks on in annoyance.

"How can you eat that? It looks disgusting!"

"Pantelis can't bear the taste of food that's been in a fridge for long," Sandra explains.

"Not just that. I don't like the color. It looks like . . . "

"Please, Pantelis!" she says and rolls her eyes.

The other fishermen dig in and are soon smacking their lips.

"I guess it just depends on what you're used to," I say, slightly amused that we have discovered each other's weak points. He doesn't like the look of gooey chocolate—I don't like the look of slimy sea urchins, but in any case, we see eye-to-eye on fish soup. The Captain relieves Pantelis of his uneaten portion of mousse and shares it with one of the children.

The mountains to the east have taken on a purplish glow, and the electric chatter of the cicadas grows more insistent. The fishermen are tired now. They have been up all night. Their expedition took them way past the uninhabited island of Psira, which you can't even see from here.

"Those cicadas are the plague of this village," says Pantelis. "You spend your vacation on a very noisy island," he says to me.

"How can a man think or rest with all that racket? There's no peace of mind in this place."

Everyone concurs, and we all go home to sleep in the hottest hours of the afternoon.

Susan Tiberghien

Yeia sas!

My husband stopped our little car, and I leaned out the window to ask a tall and imposing Cretan the way to a small Byzantine chapel marked in our guidebook. Pierre and I were vacationing for a week, away from the children, away from our work, with time for one another. And with time for discovering a faraway land, another culture, another people.

We had rented a car in bustling Iraklion and were driving around the island. We headed first along the northern shore to the far eastern point of Crete and its beaches studded with palm trees. The tempo changed centuries when we stopped at the old Toplou

Monastery, where one lone monk welcomed us. We drove south and continued along the coast to Phaistos, with its magnificent palace, considered to be the finest of all Minoan palaces, dating back to 2000 BC. At sunset we stood almost alone on the ancient ruins overlooking the immense Mediterranean.

We were now in the middle of the island, high in the hills, close to Kallikrates, where dittany and other wild herbs burst into pink blossoms in early spring. It was in these flowering fields that Zeus, disguised as a light chestnut-colored bull, courted the beautiful Europa. The myth describes how Zeus stole her away from her fair companions to take her to Crete, his own island, where she would bear him glorious sons, there in the meadows of flowering dittany high above the sea. We gathered handfuls of the aphrodisiac pink flower, perfuming our arms and saving some to make tea during the cold winters back home.

Our imposing Cretan was dressed all in black—high leather boots, wide breeches fitted at the knee, a hand-woven buttoned shirt with long sleeves. He stood strong and straight, holding on to a heavy cane. He had thick gray hair and the noble face of Cretan men, the men Henry Miller described as the most handsome in the world.

I first tried in English, then in French, to make myself understood. He shook his head. I tried again, regretting that I did not know his language.

"No Greek?" he asked.

"No Greek," I replied with an apology, but I held out the guidebook and pointed to the picture of the Byzantine chapel we wanted to visit.

He came close and looked at the book. Then he nodded and motioned to the back of our small rental car, proposing to show us the way. I pushed aside the paper bags of olives, goat cheese, the loaf of bread and bottle of Minos rosé that were to be our picnic. Our newly appointed guide folded himself in half and fitted snugly into the back of our little car.

He led us up a narrow dirt track, past a few farms, over a green hilltop, and on to another hilltop where he told us to stop and follow him on foot. We started out, walking behind him, as he led us into old, grayish green olive groves. The gnarled branches were stooped with age. Worn nets were spread over the ground to catch the last small, purple olives. There was no visible path, but our guide knew his way.

He walked steadily, and we followed, bending to pass under the low branches, stepping carefully over the nets. He slowed when he sensed we were having trouble keeping up with his sure-footed pace. We continued close behind him. Then he stopped and lifted his walking stick to point out the chapel we had seen in our book. The red sun-baked roof was half covered with vegetation, and the white walls were almost buried in the ground. We would never have recognized the chapel without our Cretan guide. We walked closer. The door was open.

Inside the dusky church, candlewicks flickered in front of ancient icons darkened from centuries of candlelight. Behind the stone altar were faded red and blue frescoes from the fourteenth century. Scenes of the Last Supper, the Garden of Gethsemane, and the Crucifixion wavered on the rounded wall. Earlier visitors had come before us that day, lighting the way. We rested a moment, letting our eyes grow accustomed to the candlelight and the darkness.

Our guide found a thin crooked candle in a tin can, lit the wick from one of the candles already burning, and placed it near the others in front of an icon of the Virgin Mary with the infant Jesus in her arms.

"The Panayia," he said, bowing his head.

Pierre and I copied his example, each taking a candle, lighting it, and finding room for it in front of the Blessed Virgin. Her regard was directly upon us. The regard of the infant Jesus was upon his mother. We stood together, next to our guide, for a long moment in silence.

I regretted once again not knowing Greek. I wished to say a short prayer aloud, to start alone and then hear our guide join in, listening to his voice. I wanted to ask him how he saw the Panayia, the Blessed Virgin, in his faith. I had to content myself with his attitude of respect and silence.

When we went back out into the sunshine, waves of heat were rising from the white walls of the chapel. We retraced our steps under the tangled branches of the olive trees. Our guide slowed his pace, asking us questions, using both English and Greek words. He nodded when he learned that we lived with our children in Switzerland, that our oldest child was married, and that we were soon to be grandparents.

"Good," he said. "For you good."

We waited.

"For me, not good."

"For you?" we asked.

"For me bad. The war. Dachau three years." He held up his hand showing three of his fingers.

We walked a bit in silence.

"My one child killed here. The war. She fifteen." He held up once again his hand, showing five fingers three times.

Slowly we learned that his village had once been large and prosperous. Then the war came, and the Germans, and the fighting. And the death of his daughter. The men were taken to Dachau. The barns, the homesteads, the fields were burned. There was no longer a village. The remaining women and children held on to small homesteads scattered out over the mountainside.

It was springtime and bushels of blossoming dittany rolled down the hillsides. But soon the pink flowers would dry under the hot sun, the green plants would turn brown and disappear under the hungry herds of goats and sheep. It would then be difficult to imagine the same hills as the blossoming love bed of Zeus and Europa. It would be easier to see them as the scarred battlefields of World War II.

When we arrived back at the car, our guide invited us to follow him to his house so that he could offer us some food and drink.

"You, friends," he said, pointing back and forth to us, to him, to us.

We accepted, and let our new friend direct us over another dirt track to the top of a hill where his house stood close to the crest. We left the car on the side of the road and took our time walking toward his house. The brick walls were whitewashed. The wooden door was hewn and chiseled by hand. He told us that most of the house had burned during the war. When he returned from Dachau, he rebuilt the gutted portions with fresh bricks he fired in a makeshift kiln. The courtyard was swept clean. There was a stone oven in the corner where he baked his own bread. From close to the front door, looking back, we could see far into the distance fields of wildflowers descending in the direction of the sea.

Inside were two rooms—the kitchen and his bedroom. His wife had died many years ago, and he lived alone. On the wall over his bed hung his daughter's gun, the one she had used while fighting with the guerrillas against the Germans not far from his farmstead.

Next to the gun was a blurred black-and-white photo of his daughter. He wanted us to look at it. The glazed surface was cracked. She was wearing a schoolgirl's smock, checkered once in bright colors. She was smiling.

The gun and the photo were all that adorned the wall.

We returned to the kitchen. Our host spread out a clean white cloth on the kitchen table and told us to sit down. There were two chairs.

"Me, how old?" he asked.

"Seventy," we guessed.

He shook his head. "Eighty-five!" He traced the numbers on my husband's hand. He had been my husband's age when he was taken to Dachau.

We watched as he took out plates, knives, forks, glasses and put them in place on the table. He handed each of us a white, folded napkin, and with another he polished the glasses. Next he brought a dish of small red tomatoes and some feta, his own goat cheese, served with little dark olives. He got a bread board and cut thick slices of a dark loaf of brown bread that he had baked in the outside oven.

Then he reached for a bottle of ouzo on the shelf by the window and filled our glasses. The aroma of the pungent aniseed spirit wrapped us together.

"*Yeia sas!*" said our friend, downing his glass.

"*Yeia sas!*" we answered.

We stayed with our host until early evening. We took photos outside in the courtyard. Then it was time to leave. We promised to send a card from Switzerland, with copies of the photos.

We still had the most impressive of the Cretan ruins to visit, the Palace of Knossos, discovered by Sir Arthur Evans at the end of the nineteenth century. This is the palace of King Minos, who built the famous labyrinth to house the mythical Minotaur.

We had saved Knossos to visit for the end of our week. We spent an entire day there, following the itinerary laid out to help visitors find their way through the 1,200 rooms. Many of the walls have been rebuilt and repainted, bright blues and reds; columns of tree trunks have been put back in place and painted bright red. Superb frescoes of dancers, acrobats, and wild bulls adorn the hallways.

The next day we flew home to Geneva. We mailed a postcard and photos to our Cretan host. We remember bustling Herakleion, the lone monk at Toplou Monastery, the ruins of Phaistos. We remember brilliant reds and blues of Knossos. But our memories return always to the hills near Kallikrates. To the blossoming dittany and to the Cretan who became our friend and welcomed us to his home. To the black-and-white photo of his daughter. To the goat cheese and his homemade dark bread. To the three glasses of ouzo. *"Yeia sas!"* To friendship!

Davi Walders

Rhodes's Lost Little Jerusalem

My husband and I sit on the marble bench in the courtyard of Kahal Shalom Synagogue in Rhodes. After rushing through crowded streets of this largest island of the Dodecanese searching for the synagogue, we rest in the shade a moment before entering. I let my eyes adjust from the dazzling sunlight.

Officially the sunniest place in Europe, Rhodes has already won my heart with its roses, the crenellated towers of the palace and city walls, and the clear azure water of the Aegean. I've wandered through the Palace of the Grandmaster, built by the Knights of Saint John, and seen the beautiful mosaic floors that Mussolini, who briefly used the palace as a vacation retreat, had installed. I've stood on the medieval city walls overlooking the sea. But I've decided to pass up the island's many other attractions—the aquarium, art galleries, shops, and restaurants. Even the beaches. I have only ten days in Greece, which is not much time for a place with so much history, so much beauty. And I am most interested in the story of Greek Jewry, an important chapter of which is set here on Rhodes, the island of roses.

The first Jews came to Rhodes from the Holy Land, possibly as slaves, possibly as traders. As early as the first century BCE, the Apostle Paul found active Jewish communities throughout the Greek islands, including Rhodes. The earliest Jews, who called themselves Romaniots, were influenced by Greek culture and language. Another influx of Jews, invited by Sultan Bayazid II to settle in Turkey, came east from Spain and Portugal after the expulsions and Inquisition of the fifteenth century. The newcomers brought with them Sephardic culture, including the Ladino language. During the twentieth century, the Jewish community of Rhodes exceeded 4,000. Until the Nazis.

The synagogue is located in a shady courtyard in the old part of Rhodes, just beyond a city square where a fountain splashes. The square has been renamed the Square of the Jewish Martyrs and contains a monument to the tragic story of the island's deported Jews.

I can see the carved wood *bimah* (*tevah* in Ladino, or raised platform in English) in the center of the synagogue and the ornate crystal chandeliers hanging from the ceiling, but I prefer to sit and watch the light coming through vine leaves trellised above the courtyard. There is a lot to take in. After all, this is the oldest standing synagogue in Greece. Built in 1577, its high arches tower over black and white pebbles set in intricate *cohlocki* (mosaics) beneath my feet.

A carved marble plaque with many names hangs to the right of the door like a huge mezuzah. I read the names: Amato, Ascher, Capelouto, Rahamim, Soulam, and so many others. The plaque is in French: *En mémoire des deux mille martyrs de la communauté juive* (In memory of two thousand martyrs from the Jewish community). It was placed here by a survivor, honoring his parents, sister, and all those of the Rhodes community who did not survive the Nazi roundups and deportations that decimated the Jewish Greek population. In 1940, 77,000 Jews lived in Greece. Only 10,000 to 15,000 survived the Holocaust. Of the almost 2,000 Rhodians who were deported, only 151 survived.

A young man wearing a *kippah* (small head covering) on his head darts in and out of the synagogue. Sent by the Athens Jewish community, he acts as caretaker and answers visitors' questions during the busy summer months. I watch him check information with a woman who sits on the marble bench. She is thin, elegantly dressed, and has short brown hair and a quick smile. She sees me writing and asks quietly where I am from. "Maryland," I tell her, "near Washington, D.C."

"I'm Sarah," she says. "I was born here." She points down the small street beside us. She betrays only a hint of accent in her soft-spoken voice. "I come back from New York every summer to help out at the synagogue." I'm afraid to hear her answer, but I say, "I hope you left before the Nazis came."

"No," she says. "I was here. Right over there is where they herded everyone." She points toward the square behind us where the fountain splashes. I ask whether she wants to talk, letting her know I don't want to intrude. She nods and begins telling her story, the story of Rhodian Jews, Rhodeslis, as they call themselves.

Before the war, this was a well-known Jewish community. There were four synagogues, and the Juderia was an immaculate, whitewashed, bustling neighborhood. Women baked sweet pastries and marzipan for the holidays. Before the holidays, the community washed the streets together and made sure that the synagogues sparkled. One of the oldest and proudest communities of the Diaspora, Rhodes was called Little Jerusalem. By spring 1944, the Nazis occupied the island, and on July 20, they rounded up the entire Jewish community, telling them to bring their jewels and money because they were to be transported to another island. After being herded without food or water onto small boats that took more than a week to reach the mainland, Sarah and the other Jews from Rhodes and Kos were crowded into the SS prison camp at Haidari. Sarah says quietly, "Men and women begged for water, but were thrown gasoline by cruel SS guards. Many of our older neighbors died."

Sarah and her sister were sent to Auschwitz where, she says, "I might not have survived except for the blessing of Madame Katz." She explains that if you couldn't understand what the Nazis demanded in German, they would beat you to death or send you to the gas chambers. Madame Katz translated the commands for Sarah, her sister, and some twenty other grateful Rhodeslie girls. She stood guard over them throughout the tortured months in Auschwitz and the terrifying death march to Dachau. They reached Dachau in April 1945, the day before the camp was liberated by the Allies. Then came the months of regaining enough strength to reenter a world of loss.

"How could you come back here?" I ask.

"It was horrible the first years," she says, "but I had no choice. It was my home. It gets a bit easier each year."

I ask my husband to take a picture of us. More than two hours have passed, and I still haven't gone into the synagogue. "I have to go in," I say, although I want to stay beside Sarah.

"Go," she says, "you must see it."

Another woman, who has apparently overheard our conversation, bends over toward us and says to Sarah, "Thank you."

"For what?" Sarah turns to her and asks.

"For surviving! I just hope you've had a good life—after all you went through," says the stranger before entering the synagogue. Sarah smiles a bit, does not respond. I too keep silent, although I resent the interruption and the shallowness of the remark.

"I've got to go in. Will you still be here?" I ask.

"I don't know," she says.

I walk through the synagogue, stand before the intricate carvings, gaze up at the chandeliers glistening in the afternoon light. Soft maroon velvet curtains protect the synagogue's Torahs. I stop a moment and say Kaddish, the prayer for the dead. It is the least I can do after Sarah's story.

I wander into a side room that has been converted into a small museum. Photographs of pre-war life in Rhodes show laughing young men and women, groups singing on the beach, wedding pictures of handsome couples. I climb the stairs to glimpse at the women's section, but I am anxious to get back to Sarah.

When I return to the courtyard, she is gone. No one seems to know where. But I have the photograph. My husband hands me the digital camera. She is smiling with her arm around me. I can still feel her presence.

I sit a moment longer, not yet ready to leave. No Colossus of Rhodes saved the Jews; no towers of the city walls protected them; no Knights of Rhodes came to their rescue; the approaching Allies never even dropped a pamphlet of warning. Here at the very end of the war, the Nazis, already losing, would not stop killing Jews. Most Greek Jews were murdered. The 151 survivors at Rhodes were barely a remnant of the former community of almost 2,000.

Now only thirty Jews live on the island. The twenty girls that Madame Katz mothered are scattered, and Madame Katz recently died. That vibrant community is memory. But Kahal Shalom, Holy Congregation of Peace, still stands, restored and cared for with the support of American Express and the World Monuments Fund . . . and Sarah and other survivors.

And Rhodeslis and visitors from all over the world come back. I was fortunate to come at just the right moment to sit beside a brave survivor and hear fragments of a tragic history. Sarah's story is one of loss and lifelong commitment to step through the pain, and on to the worn stones of the *cohlocki* and testify. Sarah's story is what the Jews of Rhodes call a *cantica*—a Ladino song, filled with love and longing. Sarah's story is a love story about a sun-splashed island and the shadow of its lost community.

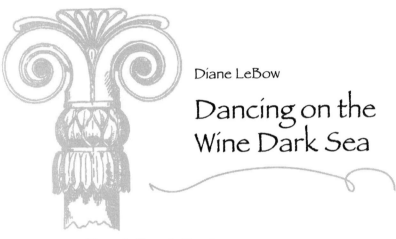

Diane LeBow

Dancing on the Wine Dark Sea

Homeric *Hymn to Demeter:*

I begin to sing of Demeter, the holy goddess with the beautiful hair. And her daughter, Persephone, too. The one with the delicate ankles, whom Hades seized. She was given away by Zeus, the loud-thunderer, the one who sees far and wide. Demeter did not take part in this, she of the golden double-axe, she who glories in the harvest. Persephone was having a good time, along with the daughters of Okeanos, who wear their girdles slung low.

(Composed circa seventh century BCE)

On our first morning in Greece, my friend Gloria and I went down to breakfast on the outdoor terrace of the Athens Hilton. Facing my eggs Benedict, all I wanted to do was lie flat on the cool terrace floor. So I did.

Waiters in white coats discreetly stepped around me, perhaps interpreting this action as eccentric American behavior. The Greek fascist regime was in full force then, and people tended to mind their own business. Gloria and I attributed my wave of nausea to bad airplane food. We proceeded to plan the rest of our trip: first by bus to visit important sites, then by sea to Mykonos and Crete.

I had just broken up with the man for whom I had left my husband. Perhaps the anxiety of learning to live the single life was stressing my system. When Gloria, a colleague at the California college where I taught, suggested a trip to Greece, I thought what better way to mend a broken heart and move on with life.

Both of us were steeped in Greek literature and history. But in the fertile lands that spawned the beginnings of our civilization, our *dimokratia*, and stories of randy gods and goddesses, I could not have guessed at the irony of my ongoing queasiness.

Our first stop was the famous amphitheater of Epidaurus, an easy day trip from Athens. We also visited Mycenae from where

Agamemnon departed for the Trojan War after he sacrificed his daughter, Iphigenia, so the gods would turn up the winds to fill his sails. His wife, Clytemnestra, was not pleased, took a lover during his ten-year absence, and murdered Agamemnon in the bath after he returned. Breaking up with my husband and now-ex-boyfriend seemed much less dramatic from this perspective.

Epidaurus was both a healing center—where Asklipios, son of Apollo, cured the ill from all over Greece—and one of the world's oldest theaters. I hoped a visit there would cure my continuing nausea. Following in the footsteps of millions, we climbed high up in the enormous amphitheater that once held 10,000 spectators and tested its legendary acoustics. Our tour guide, so far below on the stage that she seemed a tiny speck, dropped a drachma, and we heard its distinct ping as it hit the stone floor. Then she tore a Kleenex tissue, and, yes, we could hear that as well. We were sitting in what would have been, no doubt, the poor people's seats. I thought about the challenge of getting acoustics right in contemporary theaters and wondered about the many mysteries we still can learn from the ancient Greeks. Beyond the stage and backdrop (the *skini*), mountains rose and clouds floated in a blue sky. These ancient theaters were built to remind us of the connections among our temporal world, nature, and the spheres of the gods.

The next day we took a bus fourteen miles east of Athens to Eleusis, site of the Mysteries, which date back to 2000 BC and earlier. Believed to have come from Egypt via Crete, the cult of

Isis—the Earth goddess—later was worshipped as Demeter and finally the Virgin Mary. My low-grade sickness continued, as I stumbled up and down ancient stairs, soaked in the heat and odors of summer vegetation. Poppies dotted the surrounding slopes, and cicadas buzzed in the overgrown bushes.

I had read that this area was once the terminus of a biannual procession that began in Athens along what was called the Sacred Way. Anyone could participate, as long as he was not a barbarian (i.e., someone who doesn't speak Greek) and had not committed blood crimes. As they walked, people, especially prostitutes, called out dirty words and obscene jokes. The overall celebration marked Demeter's reunion with her daughter, Persephone, when she returned from her six-month annual sojourn with Hades, god of the underworld. During her daughter's months in the underworld, Demeter was too sad to tend to fertility, hence winter set in. The ancients also reported that Persephone was reborn from her mother in the midst of huge fire and brilliant lights seen for miles around. Bulls and phalli were part of these rituals, depicted in frescoes as far away as Pompeii.

Here amid this ancient place of orgies and bloody sacrifice, the thought that I could I be pregnant flashed through my mind. If so, what would I do? I was on my own. I couldn't afford to stop my work, both teaching college and training horses. No one was going to take care of me. I wondered if I would be able to get an early flight home.

After I'd vomited over some of the most fertile sites of Western culture—Delphi, Epidaurus, Mycenae—we decided to save money by taking the ferry over from Piraeus to Crete. The *meltemi*, the hot winds of August, blew heavy on the Aegean. Because of these relentless winds, the ancient Greeks avoided open sea travel as much as possible during this time of year. We soon discovered why. What was typically a nine-hour overnight voyage took almost fifteen hours. I lay on the center of the top deck, watching Orion and the seven sisters rock back and forth overhead. After downing seasickness pills, which had little or no effect, I finally read the directions and noticed a bold-print warning: "Do not take during pregnancy as may cause birth defects to fetus." I began to panic at the thought that I was now carrying a deformed fetus.

When we reached the terra firma of Crete, we checked into our economy hotel. Just down the street was the Palace of Knossos, which we visited the next day, marveling at the flush toilet that the Minoan queen enjoyed four thousand years ago. I wondered what her life was like. Having a daughter to carry on a woman's lineage was central in this matrilineal culture.

That evening Gloria announced she was leaving to tour with a professor from Germany she had met during our ferry crossing. "There's no point in my staying with you," she said. "You're sick and can't do anything. I may as well have fun."

I felt abandoned but decided it was time to make some decisions. Changing my Pan Am return ticket home, I booked a flight from Iraklion to Athens, happily forfeiting my return ferry ticket. Back in California, I was grateful that abortions had just become legal.

Song of the Sirens, from Homer's *The Odyssey:*

Draw near . . . illustrious Odysseus, flower of the Achaean chivalry, and bring your ship to rest that you may hear our voices. No seaman ever sailed his black ship past this place without listening to the sweet voice that flow from our lips, and none that listened has not been delighted and gone on a wiser man.

"My darling Aphrodite, I love you. Will you marry me?" The handsome Greek restaurant owner on Santorini pleaded with my eighty-year-old mother as they line-danced to bouzouki music in a late-night bacchanal on a terrace overlooking the Aegean. My mother loved dancing, charming men, and living in general. After being widowed for the second time in her late seventies, she kicked up her heels and, in many ways, relished life to its fullest. During those years we traveled together frequently and had our own high-spirited odyssey around Greece.

My jaunt with my mother came years after my first inauspicious steps on Greek soil. It was natural that we finally shared Athens and the Greek isles together. Greece lived in my imagination from my earliest memories thanks to her. An avid reader and elementary-school teacher, she had read Homer's *The Iliad* and *The Odyssey* and tales from Greek mythology to me as a child. I imagined sailing the Aegean with Odysseus, visiting the lands of the Lotus Eaters and Circe and the Cyclops for myself. As a college professor, I taught Greek literature. My mother named me Diane, the Roman counterpart of Artemis, the free-spirited huntress. Artemis frolicked in the woods, surrounded by animals, without a thought to marriage or children.

Like my mythological namesake, I enjoyed my adventurous approach to life and my work with animals for many years as a professional horse trainer. Yet, sometimes I thought about what I was missing, having remained *child-free*. After all, my mother enjoyed having a daughter. I would have no daughter but would continue on my namesake's path. Like Demeter and Persephone, my mother and I were accepting of where our lives had led us.

At our hotel in Delphi, my mother telephoned my room. "Yorgos, our driver, is knocking at my hotel room door. What should I do?" she said. She had been flirting with the poor man for several days as we toured around. How could he know that she was only kidding? "Maybe you should let him in," I advised. "You've been leading him on for days now." Meanwhile I was busy with our young tour guide who was licking my cheek and nibbling my shoulder.

Mom and I sailed to Santorini, this time on the calm seas of early June. The lost Atlantis, some believe, is under the waters of Santorini's bay. We visited the archaeological excavations underway and, in the afternoon, hired a local man with a rowboat to take us to a beach I had heard about. "A nudie beach," I told my mother, who hoped to add yet another act of daring to her repertoire. On the beach, my frisky mom stripped to her white cotton underpants and bra and enjoyed splashing in the clear warm Aegean. When our oarsman and boat returned after the designated hour or two, he asked us to wade out to the boat. Seeing my mother, still in her underwear, having trouble negotiating the pebbled bottom, he jumped out, waded to shore, and, to her immense delight, scooped her up into his arms, both of them giggling their way back to the rowboat.

On our first night we had dinner at an open-air taverna, with the full moon illuminating the Aegean and the island's chalk-white cliffs. We drank ouzo and retsina, ate souvlaki and *tzatziki*. "Did you know," a fisherman at our table asked, "that in the old days if a wife was rebellious and refused to have sex with her husband, he would be advised to rub her gently with olive oil for seven days? After that time, she would become sweet and compliant." He winked and passed me the olive oil for my salad. Winking back, I doused my tomato, feta, cucumber, and olives with the ancient golden remedy.

Musicians on the *bouzouki, karamoudzes, baglama,* and *daouli* drums began to play their irresistible music. Soon we were all line dancing. Several women said, "We'll teach you an ancient women's dance. This used to be the only dance women were allowed. It was for widows who danced their way off the edge of a cliff." I looked skeptically at the drop at the end of the restaurant terrace. "We won't do that tonight though," they assured me.

I remembered twenty years earlier during the fascist regime when I first visited Greece. Gloria and I got up to dance at a taverna in the Plaka in Athens. We were the only ones on the floor, proudly showing off the steps we had recently learned at our lessons at a San Francisco Greek restaurant. We'd been told that we might have a problem if we danced in Greece. When a handsome man approached us, Gloria said to me, "See, it's okay for us to be dancing." He came so close that I could sniff the ouzo on his breath: "Seet down," he snarled. "Women don't dance in Greece."

That same night Gloria and I did enjoy the plate-bashing party. Some people at the restaurant invited us to join a birthday celebration. Shades were pulled down on all the windows. "It's against the law these days to break plates," they whispered. Suddenlyeveryone jumped up and started dancing and dashing china to the floor until we were crunching broken pottery with every step.

Here on Santorini, although there was no plate-smashing, the chef appeared from the kitchen and began dancing alone in the middle of the floor. We all clapped, urging him to still-higher leaps and slaps of hand on heel. He did several backflips, then tore off one of his sleeves, placed it on his head like a chef's hat. "I hope he doesn't sweat in our *tzatziki*," said my mom. Seeing her gyrating in her seat, the chef urged her onto the dance floor. He tore off his other sleeve and placed it on her head.

Meanwhile the charming Adonis of a jeweler, Thanassis, whom we had met earlier that day when we were looking at traditional Greek key design necklaces, joined our table. He and I had made a tentative date as we left his shop. I slipped away for a tryst at his apartment where I learned that it is not only thousands of years of philosophy that the Greeks are adept at. No wonder, I thought, that Lysistrata and her friends wanted their men back in their beds. As the rosy-fingered dawn broke over the white cliffs and blue waters of Santorini, Thanassis drove me back to my hotel where I caught a few hours' sleep before my mom and I sailed off on the early morning ferry to Páros for our next island adventure.

Both my mother and I disliked early mornings, but this one was special as the sun peeked over the blue Aegean and then rose up as we sailed into its path. "What a magical trip this is," said my mom. "I'm so lucky to have such a wonderful daughter."

"Ditto, for me," I said. "How many mothers would be the belle of the ball at a Greek taverna and then not mind when I run off with the most handsome Greek on the island?"

"I was only concerned that I didn't have to take this ferry by myself if you didn't show up. I'm not sure where we're going next!"

Five years later, I was back in Greece, this time accompanied by my mother's ashes. My plan was to sprinkle them in the waters off Santorini, a place where we had both had such fun together. I lay awake in my hotel in Athens, thinking about my mother's recent death. I was in the same hotel, not far from the Plaka with a view of the Acropolis, where my mother and I stayed as we began that last madcap voyage together. I thought about my mother reading Greek myths to me at my bedside so many years ago. Now I was returning to Greece to scatter her ashes in Homer's "wine dark sea."

So many memories here. Greece, ancient and modern, had intertwined itself throughout my life. My mother's death marked the end of my family. Yes, I was alone but my life was a satisfying one—and there were lots of adventures still to come.

Suddenly my bed began to jump around the room. The hotel rocked, and when I looked out the window, it seemed that the Acropolis itself was undulating. In the morning, I learned that a major earthquake jolted Greece, the epicenter was near Sparta. Hotels had fallen over and hundreds of people had been killed. Having never felt earthquakes anywhere other than my home in San Francisco, I recalled both the fragility and continuity of our world.

Since my mother had loved her time in Greece and flirted shamelessly with every handsome young Greek who crossed her path, I felt she'd like being out there in that clear blue water where new generations of young Greeks would be frolicking. Some friends and I chanted a poem I had written for the occasion, called "Hymn to Audrey":

You danced music into my life:
I send you dancing on all the seas and beaches
of the world.
You gave me peace.
I wish you peace with the winds and the waves
and the seas
which are always and everywhere.

As I freed her ashes into the azure water, the calm bay suddenly sizzled and glittered with the sparkles of a million diamonds. "Wow, what is happening?" one of my companions gasped. This was the stuff of Greek myths, and we looked at each other wide-eyed. Very possibly by now my mother was playing the coquette with Charon, as he ferried her across the Styx, and was enticing Hades himself into a line dance.

That night I caught the midnight ferry from Santorini to continue my own odyssey on whatever island lay ahead.

Ronna N. Welsh

Hooked on Octopus in Molyvos

Sometimes if you chew an octopus tentacle just so, you can loosen a sucker from its skin. You can toss it around in your mouth, as you would a Jujube, and maybe slip your tongue into it, as you would a back molar. You can bite into it hesitatingly, because you don't like the thought of eating something akin to an orifice. It chews like the rest of the tentacle, resistant but ultimately pliant, and delicious—so delicious!—and you are relieved.

The octopus lurks in water's shadows, but also thrives conspicuously on land. It has steadfast publicists in Greek tourism, mythology, and art, popping up in island postcards, in children's stories, and on pottery dating back millennia. Grilled, especially, it rouses the Greek appetite for ouzo and conversation. It is the pride of Greek fishermen to catch one, especially a *big* one, and of the islands' cooks to turn it tender.

The *ohtapodi* that arrive by cart in front of the Captain's Table—a typically small restaurant toward the far end of Molyvos's modest harbor—are big even by my chef standards, with heads the size of Yukon potatoes and, held aloft, tentacles falling seventeen inches toward the ground. Like most of the octopuses found around Greece, these are mud brown, matching the sea rocks they cleverly hide between. They appear a mottled, dusty purple against the Mediterranean sky. Their eyes like glossy white marbles bulge from the sides of their heads, only slightly bigger than the biggest sucker, which are also, underneath a translucent sheath of skin, round and stark white. Each tentacle wields about seventy-five pairs of suckers, lined in symmetrical double rows and progressively shrinking in size from the octopus's head to the straw-thin tip. Tentacles occasionally contort like a broken bone or twist like licorice, and grow fat and thin alternately. Like a tree's rings, an octopus's tentacles document a history of environmental change with their size and shape. When the cephalopod loses part of a tentacle in a mishap or fierce contest with death, it grows back like hair after chemotherapy. The regenerated part inevitably looks different and weaker. But it crisps up nicely on the grill.

Melinda contends that Theo, her husband, grills the best octopus in Molyvos, if not the whole island of Lesvos. She told me this months after I had initially contacted her, looking for an offbeat place overseas to apprentice as a cook. "We are just a small Greek restaurant on the island of Lesvos, and I feel sure that there is nothing I can teach you," she wrote me. "It is precisely because you are a small restaurant on the island of Lesvos . . ." I protested, earnest in my quest for authentic Greek food.

The Captain's Table, like most restaurants in this modest but stunning and busy harbor, caters to well-mannered northern European and Australian tourists. But the Captain's Table stands out for its grilled octopus alone, which, Melinda purports, is worth traveling far to taste.

Hand-catching an octopus is a testament to Greek virility. Octopuses can frustrate the strongest grip. If tugged at by their heads, they will grab on to nearby rocks and let themselves be torn to pieces before being fished out. And they are playful; they know how to taunt. Theo remembers seeing an octopus sunning itself in shallow water, its head bobbing above the surface like a buoy, like a dare. They are solitary, too, preferring to live alone rather than fight another octopus for territory. To kill an octopus quickly, one must bash its head and break the radula, a thin bone located where a forehead might be. In the tallest tales, such as those that Theo tells, you can stare the octopus in the face and bite this bone in two by sinking your teeth right between its eyes.

Tour guides suggest you then tenderize the octopus by hitting it on the rocks, in the company of bronzed, shirtless men wading in knee-high water, grunting hard forty times.

"More like a hundred," Theo says. At least for the big ones, but there aren't many of those left. Do this while hordes of Danish tourists shoot reams of video.

Kids fish for octopus, too. It is a rite of passage. They go for the small ones whose tentacles are no longer than a child's outstretched arms, heeding tales of octopuses who will wrap around a vulnerable little throat. But to most fishermen, the suckers pose the greatest danger, pulling at their sun-coarse skin, adhering even after the octopus has died, and branding them with welts when they free themselves from the tenacious seal. I hear tales of octopuses near Australia—inhabiting the waters with sharks and other menacing creatures—that will bite humans. The one Theo now holds, caught for him by good luck in a fisherman's net, is petite and passive by comparison.

At the Captain's Table, we dismember and clean the octopus, a tentacle at a time, and set the limbs aside. We take what remains of the head, dispensing first with the innards and mouth, leaving a translucent, torn sac that resembles a busted PinkyBall. We rinse it well and toss it whole into a stew of scorpion fish, potatoes, tomatoes, carrots, onions, and celery—in Greece, always celery—that's been long-cooking on the stove. It is a *catch-all* classic.

Into a pot of simmering salt water, we add any brutally mangled octopus legs. At dinner, Theo will serve them at room temperature, poached tender as young chicken, with warm dried-oregano vinaigrette. The rest, to the obvious delight of guidebook editors and camera-toting tourists, we hang to dry on a clothesline in the sun, alongside fillets of salted white tuna, splayed open with shaved twigs.

Melinda shuts down the kitchen around three thirty, after preparing stews, soups, dips, and sauces, and feeding her kids, who drop by at irregular intervals.

One afternoon during a break, I walk the arc of the harbor wall and watch the fishermen still busy on their boats, ignoring the work hiatus on land. I pass Vangelis, the harbor's popular bouzouki musician, who pulls his modest fishing boat up to the restaurant's dock. His dog, Barney, released for the day from sea-faring duties, lies on the dock, aloof to the dozens of homeless cats that tirelessly cruise the harbor. Instead, his gaze fixes on me. I stop to scratch Barney behind the ears where he seems to want it.

Vangelis smiles, pleased with his dog's magnetism and happy for the attention it inadvertently draws to him. He recognizes me as the lone American who disappears into the Captain's Table each morning, swims with Melinda and Theo's children in the afternoon, and dines with the family at night. At first, he takes me for an au pair, which frustrates me. My role here, though, is admittedly ill-defined; I am at once a cook, caretaker, and guest.

I tell Vangelis about cleaning octopus that morning and my earnest yearning to catch one. Despite my protestations, Vangelis considers me a tourist full of fanciful ideas about a lazy day at sea. So I don't tell him how this would be only my second time fishing, still trying to forget my first, a scarring event that involved a Pennsylvania lake, the moon, worm goo, and a mean boyfriend. To be fair, I don't consider Vangelis the quintessential fisherman—there are other, more impressive operators around. But he speaks some English and is otherwise approachable, flirtatious even. So he's probably my only way off shore. We agree to meet at the boat the next morning. It is my fragile hope that the sea—the harbor's backbone, home to the alluring octopus—will satisfy my search for a true sense of place.

Early the next day, the harbor is still, the last of the café employees having retired a few hours before. I am flush with the anticipation of a fishing venture and greet Vangelis's dog eagerly at his boat's bow. His chest and head are thrust forward, as a ship's bust. His tail hangs tautly between muscular hind legs, tensed in a slight curl at the tip. I climb onto the boat and sit opposite Vangelis under the slight khaki canopy. It is roomy enough for a man, his dog, a curious stranger, and their catch.

A much larger fishing boat pulls up to dock next to us, back already from a full morning's work. Two men begin to untangle their yellow nets, hand over hand, inspecting them for holes, unknotting snagged seaweed. The nets pile up like spaghetti as high as their heads. They cover them with a cruddy Turkish rug, pause to light a cigarette, and piss into the sea.

A champion of our casual venture, Vangelis claims we're going where the best octopuses are, and he shows me a red rubber crab with hooks to catch the biggest. He moves his boat, pale compared with the royal blue and crimson boats surrounding it, out of the harbor. The cliffs rise up from the water around tiny Platyialos beach, a small patch of sand accessible only by sea. Over the years, this beach has seen its share of capsized rafts of immigrants from Turkey, Iraq, and Iran; it lies empty and quiet today.

When we reach water that is ten meters deep, Vangelis shuts off the noisy, polluting motor. We have exhausted our kindly, unmemorable chatter and sit quietly, save for Vangelis's whistling. He drops some fishing line, hooked to bright plastic bait, lightweight enough to float near the surface. It trails behind as we drop two clunky blue oars into the water. Vangelis paddles us a bit out of wind. The double-decker *Mercury Express* ferries by. By habit, Vangelis checks his watch and lights a cigarette then drops anchor. Barney and I stare dreamily ahead at the reflections cast by seabirds on the water. We watch the line sink, untroubled by the ferry's lingering wake.

Vangelis improvises a fishing rod for me, first looping a few feet of additional line around my index finger, then draping it over my forearm. He weighs the line with a beak hook, a bit of jellyfish, which he steals from the sea's surface, and the red rubber crab. As Theo says, "Octopus like crab."

Opa! He flings the bait into the sea.

The sun intensifies as we sit in silence, most other boats having already docked for the day. I imagine the crowds gathering at the harbor, breaking the morning's quiet spell, Theo running errands, Melinda on the phone, the baby on the porch. Melinda would be talking about the bread order or to her mother about lunch with the kids. Likely, she'd mention her curious American visitor who accompanied *that character* Vangelis out to sea.

I look up to see passersby stare from their perches on the stone wall in front of the small grocery where I have sat many mornings, eating yogurt and watching the boats arrange themselves on the water. People point their cameras toward us, our solitary efforts rendered quaint by a photograph's willful frame. I feel a bit silly keeping company with this fisherman in his scantily equipped boat, which, I now notice, has no cooler for keeping fish, let alone storing a great octopus. I feel a surging disenchantment and wonder how we must amuse the other fishermen, not to mention the stealthy cephalopod. Has this venture to sea been no more than a charade?

When we pull into the harbor two long hours later, we are greeted by the Sea Horse Hotel's manager at work refilling coffee for breakfasting guests. He smiles at us, calling out false niceties. Also, a fifty-ish, spectacled Danish man, with whom I occasionally share drinks, smiles delightedly and waves with his newspaper from a café nearby. With goodwill, I muster a false enthusiasm and beckon him to the dock. I hold my arms out to say *"This* big!" while stepping in front of our paltry catch, one *psari*, a fish no more than four inches long and one inch wide, preempting anyone mocking our failure to nab anything else.

Our fish has four wispy, translucent beige fins and scales of tan with dark brown spots, a spiny crown on its head, and a pink mouth open as wide as a grape. It is no bigger than the fish caught by Kimon, Melinda and Theo's seven-year-old son, and his friends with their minirods from the dock. Sadly, it is more bait than catch, more pet than meal. Because the boat has no fish storage tank, my souvenir swims in a small plastic bucket, which Vangelis has emptied of tackles.

Our audience appears to restrain a snicker until, as if on cue, the fish floats up in the water, dead.

I am about to dump my *psari* overboard, feeling silly that I had held on to it at all and sillier for thinking I'd catch anything else. Vangelis had encouraged me to keep the fish, thinking I'd like a token from the sea. On our quixotic quest for the octopus, this was my consolation prize.

"Not dead! Not dead!" Vangelis tickles the fish's gills with the pad of a finger. He thrusts it toward me and instructs me to resuscitate.

"Huh?"

Vangelis has proven to be kind-spirited, and I trust that his intent to save the fish is not meant to mock me. So, at his insistence and for the benefit of our small audience, including a trio of harbor cats, I play along, self-consciously, daring to blow at the fish's head. It doesn't flinch.

"No! No! Like this!" Vangelis pries open the fish's tiny-teeth-lined jaw and presses his own lips to it. He sucks in deeply, depleting the air in the fish's body cavity, then exhales violently, distending the fish's slippery corpse. The fish caves and expands like a vacuum bag. Vangelis carries on like this for a few minutes. It's delightfully absurd.

I glance curiously at the others, surprised to find them similarly tensed in anticipation of the fish's revival. As if to appease its hopeful audience, the fish starts to quiver reflexively.

"Vangelis! Vangelis!" I cheer, in spite of myself and now inspired by this fisherman for whom dead fish ought not be worth wasted breath. It's as if one life wasted would create an imbalance of trade.

"See," he says thoughtfully to no one in particular as he slips the *psari* into the sea, the octopus momentarily forgotten.

"Swim! Swim!" I implore, reaching into the water and grabbing the fish by the tail, propelling it forward as if to illustrate the act. The fish flits about once, twice, and then shimmies steadily. We applaud and watch the fish, reborn, swim away.

"There," he says. "See?"

Yes, now I do. The octopus, like Molyvos, has inhabited the juncture of myth and romance; it was ultimately a pawn of my imagination. But an octopus is really no more authentically *Greek* than this unimpressive little fish I caught guided by a man who could hardly earn a living at sea. Here, as anywhere, authenticity is experiential, found in fleeting, honest transactions between people, like Vangelis and me; it is not something that can be simply caught nor, by extension, cooked and consumed.

A few handshakes and we pack up unused life vests and water bottles. I head toward the restaurant, details of my excursion soon to be lost to the routine of work. When I glance back at the boat, now tied up and empty, I lose sight of our fish, my token of redemption, which has by now moved out to sea.

Tara Kolden

Bitter Oranges

In Greek mythology, the pomegranate is Persephone's undoing. Hades, god of the dead, kidnaps the maiden and takes her to his subterranean lair, which, though grim, is not completely lacking in hospitality. His servants lay out a feast for the girl, but she refuses to touch so much as a crust of bread, so unhappy is she to be in this foreign place. One of Hades's gardeners offers her the pomegranate, however, and she cannot resist the cluster of ruby seeds. She eats seven of them, and her fate is sealed: She will return home again, but be forever bound to this strange and darkly magical realm. An age-old reminder of how the sense of taste can tie us to a place.

My culinary love affair with Greece began with another forbidden fruit, but it was one I never ultimately ate; unlike Persephone, I received fair warning about its dangers. I was cautioned by an American man on my flight to Athens. "Watch out for the orange trees," he told me. "You'll see them all over the city, lining the streets." He rolled his eyes. "You can always tell the tourists. They're the ones picking the oranges and trying to eat them, right there on the sidewalk. Those oranges are the bitterest things you ever tasted."

I duly looked out for them on the taxi ride into the city. Sand-colored buildings and spike-leaved foliage in the suburbs gradually gave way to the smoggy city center, a place that seemed unlikely to foster any sort of flora, but there they were. It was mid-January and the weather was crisp, but the bitter oranges appeared to be in season. We passed dozens of the little trees, all heavy with fruit. It was the first time I had seen living, growing oranges; I was delighted. The fruits were bright and perfect, and because the trees were small, the oranges were easily within reach of passersby. I understood the temptation to take one. Their bitterness was like a tiny, dark secret, and somehow I liked them more for it.

That night at a small hotel—my first in the Mediterranean— I lounged on the rooftop terrace with an American friend. We smoked clove cigarettes and leaned against the metal railing on the edge of the roof, watching the traffic below. The cars were loud, and the air was heavy. Around us, televisions blared from the neighboring tenements and lines of pale laundry haunted the alley beside our building. We had no view of the Acropolis. But observing the long line of orange trees stretching along the street below, I felt certain I'd arrived in some sort of paradise.

We were students, my friend and I, starting out on a semester-long study program based in Athens. The curriculum was rich in art and culture, history and language: There were to be seminars conducted by some of Greece's most respected archaeologists, museum visits on the mainland and the islands, tutorials on sculpture, epigraphy, iconography. We would live in apartments scattered throughout the neighborhood of Kolonaki, where the city's flat center gave way to the steep climb of Lycabettus, a parklike peak traversed with walking paths and a small tram leading to look-out points with staggering views of the surrounding city. We were responsible for buying our own course materials and other amenities, but the study program provided us with one meal a day.

It didn't take long to discover that our education over the next few months would be as much about food as it was about academics. Students participating in the program—a hundred or so of us—had come from all over the United States, and we had chosen different areas of study. Our one great unifier was lunch. Each weekday afternoon we gathered in a dining hall on a street called Patriarchou Ioakeim, and a staff of jovial local women served us an ever-changing menu of traditional Greek food.

The meals were beautiful in their simplicity. Lunch always began with crusty bread we dressed with oil and vinegar or with *tzatziki*, a spread made of yogurt, cucumber, and garlic. A fresh salad followed. The ingredients were simple—tomatoes, cucumbers, onions, olives, and crumbled feta cheese—but their fresh flavor made the dish a show-stopper. The entree, though, was the best. Some days it was avgolemono, the tangy soup made with egg, lemon, and rice. Or pastitsio, a baked pasta dish with cheese and béchamel. Other days we were served thick wedges of spanakopita (spinach, cheese, and phyllo pastry) or helpings of moussaka, which had the layered look of lasagna but was made with eggplant, lamb, and béchamel.

Other than these lunches, we bought our own food. Tips on the best corner grocers, the best weekend produce markets, and the best tavernas quickly spread among the students. Down the street from our dining hall was a hole-in-the-wall selling gyros, and it quickly became our favorite dinner venue. Many evenings, my flatmates and I would scrape together a few drachmas and pay a visit. The menu choices were limited—lamb or pork, with *tzatziki* or without, with fries or without—but the food was cheap and delectable. Once we'd made up our minds, the owner would slice fresh-cooked meat off the rotisserie and fill small, oven-hot pitas. He came to know us well and welcomed us warmly, regardless of how little of his language we could manage.

More daunting was the weekend market, which filled the narrow streets of Kolonaki with fruit and vegetable vendors. Here we bought the ingredients for homemade salads and other dishes. The choices were overwhelming, and the competition fierce. Sellers called out the prices of cabbages, apples, lettuce. My favorite vendors were those who sold olives. They surrounded themselves with small fortresses of olive barrels, each full of a different shining variety. You had only to point, and a ladle-full of oily black, rich green, or deep mahogany-colored olives was yours. Here, too, were my bitter oranges, sold to make marmalades and other preserves.

Outside the city, more gastronomic adventures awaited. An archaeological field trip to the Peloponnese yielded more than just the opportunity to explore inside the massive walls of Mycenae. Our first night, in Nafplion, we ate octopus.

The leader of our group, an American professor, took us out for an evening meal and made sure a large dish of grilled tentacles made it to our table. "You have to eat it hot," he said, and demonstrated by popping a segment into his mouth. "Once it gets cold, it turns rubbery." Fresh from the grill, the octopus had a mild, pleasant taste. I was fascinated by the way it looked. The tentacles had been cut into innocuous, bite-size pieces before they reached us, but there was no disguising the large round suckers on each morsel. I loved it.

Dolmades—grape leaves stuffed with seasoned rice—quickly became another favorite of mine. So did souvlaki, skewers of grilled lamb served at many of our meals on the road. But Greek coffee was a harder sell. I like strong drip coffee and the occasional espresso at home, but this did little to prepare me for the concoctions we often ordered after a long Greek meal. Many times, the waiter brought us instant Nescafé, doctored with milk and sugar to create something pleasantly palatable. Other times, though, we got the real thing: thick Greek coffee that, for a beverage, came perilously close to crossing the line between a liquid and a solid. The top half of the cup was usually liquid, but below that crucial halfway point was a rich, murky sludge for which I never acquired a taste. I became skilled in sludge-avoidance and generally knew exactly how far I could dunk the accompanying cookie without coating it in a layer of sticky coffee grounds.

I discovered my favorite Greek recipe on the island of Crete. The same professor who had introduced us to octopus had our culinary well-being in mind. On a sleepy February morning before a visit to Gournia, he interrupted a lecture on ancient history and asked our driver to pull our bus onto a side street in the town of Iraklion.

The professor made sure he had our attention before beginning his explanation.

"I *strongly* recommend—" He paused for emphasis, and we all leaned a little closer to hear his next instructions. His tone suggested that our grades might depend on them"—that you walk across the street to that bakery, which is open. Do you see it? Walk over there, and ask for *bougatsa*. Say it with me, people: *bougatsa*."

Like a Greek chorus, we chanted the word. *Bougatsa*. I didn't know it then, but the word was to become my personal mantra.

Ever obedient, we filed out of the bus and across the street to find out what he was talking about. The bakery was empty of customers, but was already well stocked with the day's fresh goods. We gathered around a glass case filled with sweets: cookies, baklava, and the object of our expedition. *Bougatsa* turned out to be a large pocket of phyllo dough filled with a creamy milk custard. The woman at the counter scooped up helpings for us. As she served them, she opened up a corner of each phyllo pocket—like unmaking a tiny bed—and sprinkled cinnamon inside, then neatly folded the phyllo back into place. The portions were served to us in paper wrappers so we could eat them on the go. We clustered outside on the deserted sidewalk, and, under a sky turning pink and purple with the rising sun, we savored this impromptu breakfast. The *bougatsa* was warm, and it tasted like heaven.

This pastry became the morning staple that coffee had been at home. Although I first tasted it on Crete, I found it was available everywhere. In Athens I located bakeries near my apartment and my classes so that my favorite sweet was never far from hand.

I discovered other delicacies, however, that were strictly regional. Corfu, for example, was the kingdom of the kumquat. On a weekend trip to the island, I was assailed by kumquats the moment I stepped off the boat. I arrived early in the morning, and bought Nescafé and *bougatsa* at a small café in the ferry terminal.

As I sipped my coffee I looked around at the other items for sale. In addition to the usual supply of baked goods, candy bars, and soft drinks, there was an entire wall devoted to the kumquat—candied kumquats, pickled kumquats, kumquat preserve, kumquat sweets, kumquat liqueur. This last was bright red. I vowed to try it. Later that day, I bought some and took it back to my hotel room. It was sweet, but not particularly exciting. What it lacked in flavor it made up for in novelty. I hoped to see actual kumquat trees during my excursion, but they were not as plentiful as the orange trees of Athens.

Easter was the last holiday that fell during my stay in Greece. I spent it on the island of Santorini, where I found more new food to try. Every bakery window displayed elaborate Easter breads—loaves of braided dough with one or more red-dyed eggs placed inside them. I bought one to share with friends, and we sat on the beach of black sand and pulled apart the braids. The bread was light and slightly sweet. At a taverna on Easter Sunday, we ate dinner at an outdoor table. I ordered octopus and other seafood and dipped my bread in *tzatziki*. We lingered at the table until after dark, telling stories and feeding scraps to a cat that had wandered under our table. In the distance, lights from an Easter procession twinkled like stars.

Back in Athens, I tried to make the most of my remaining time in Greece. I returned to the Acropolis and the archaeological museum, but I also made sure to revisit my favorite tavernas. I bought apples at the street market. I put in my final order from the gyro seller down the street: two pork gyros, no *tzatziki*, extra fries. And as for my little orange trees, which seemed always to be full of fruit, I watched them go by as my taxi drove out of the city on the way back to the airport. Once, twice, I thought I saw pedestrians who had stopped to pick the fruit. *Tourists*, I thought. *Locals know better than to eat those.* But was I really so smart? I'd never tasted one, but still, like Persephone, I found myself bound to two separate worlds.

Acknowledgments

Thanks are due to all the writers who offered their fine work for consideration in this collection, many of whom are ardent supporters of Seal Press's work. It was a treat to read about so many different "Greeces," although it was impossible to include them all in this anthology. Extra thanks to the writers whose work appears here, for their deep, perceptive understanding of the country and culture of Greece, and for their ability to write sensitive, lyrical, and helpful portraits that surpass the ordinary travel story. Many thanks for their patience in reworking and tweaking their stories as needed. Big thanks to my coeditor at Seal Press, Denise Silva, for her unflagging editorial support and for keeping this project on track through its highs and lows and several curves and speed bumps. And, as always, I'm deeply grateful to Seal Press (small house, big heart) for its unrelenting quest to give readers the best work that informs women's lives.

About the Contributors

Katherina Audley, completing her informal year abroad in Crete, hitchhiked to Lanzarote, in the Canary Islands, where she spent a year learning about the time-share industry and the shadier sides of Spain and Morocco. Upon her return to the United States, Audley worked at the Exploratorium in San Francisco. In 2001, she began making extended visits to Latin America, culminating in a nine-month overland traverse of South America from Tierra del Fuego to Cartagena. She lives and writes in Portland, Oregon, and never did get her master's degree.

Ashley Black is a writer and screenwriter in San Francisco. She is currently finishing a novel situated in her beloved Epirus.

Simone Butler is a writer, astrologer, and artist who began her career as a fashion editor for *California Apparel News*. She has written about the arts for publications such as the *Los Angeles Times, San Diego Magazine,* and *The Mountain Astrologer.* She teaches treasure mapping classes at the Golden Door Spa and does private astrological consultations out of her rural hideaway in Escondido, California. Visit her at www.AstroAlchemy.com.

Alison Cadbury has had a love affair with Greece since arriving on the island of Paros by accident in September 1971. She has lived a total of six years on Paros with a few months each on Crete, Kithera, Tinos, and Chios, and a year or so in Athens. Her writings about Paros have been published in *The Georgia Review, The Missouri Review,* and *Ascent.* While studying modern Greek literature at San Francisco State University, she received a Fulbright fellowship to write a master's thesis on Modern Greek novelist Ilias Venezis. In 1995, she was awarded a fellowship by the National Endowment for the Arts to work on a book of creative nonfiction about Paros. She lives in Eugene, Oregon, where she teaches writing at a community college.

Amanda Castleman returned to Seattle after eight years in England, Italy, Greece, and Cyprus. An Italian American travel writer, she has contributed to the *International Herald Tribune,* the *Daily Mail, MSNBC, Salon, Wired,* and *Italy Daily.* Her guidebook credits include *Time Out Athens, The Rough Guide to Italy,* and *Rome and Central Italy Adventure Guide.* She holds a degree in Latin and teaches travel writing. Her website is at www.amandacastleman.com.

Cynthia Greenberg has been writing about her travels since 1973 when she studied filmmaking and photography at the American University in Rome. She put herself through school acting in spaghetti westerns and had a brief role in *The Godfather: Part II*. She hopes to publish her novel, *Burmese Jade*, based on her journeys in Thailand, Malaysia, and Burma. She received honorable mention in the 2006 *Writer's Digest* fiction competition for her short story "Fire." She lives in Marin County, California.

Linda Hefferman is a freelance writer living with her husband and two sons in Portland, Oregon. Her writing has appeared in *ByLine Magazine*, the anthology *How to Leave a Place*, and forthcoming in *Mothering* magazine. She is currently working on a technical book for the *Dummies* series and a travelogue/memoir about a year in France where her second son was born.

Tara Kolden's travel writing has appeared in anthologies published by Seal Press and Lonely Planet. She's been marooned on Skyros and romanced in Montmartre, and she's eaten haggis by choice. When not wreaking havoc in foreign territories, she makes her home in Seattle.

Linda Lappin lives in Rome. She is the author of a novel, *The Etruscan*. She directs the writing program of the Centro Pokkoli in Vitorchiano, Italy, a medieval village near Rome. For more on her and the program, see www.pokkoli.org and www.linda lappin.net.

Diane LeBow lives in San Francisco and has published stories in *Salon; VIA* magazine; *Travelers' Tales Guides; France, A Love Story; Foreign Affairs: Erotic Travel Tales; B for savvy brides* magazine; *Skirt!* magazine; and numerous national newspapers and magazines. Recently her photography won the Bay Area Travel Writer Association Silver Award. She travels the globe and has spent time with Afghan women, Libyans, the Hopi, Amazon people, Tuvans, Mongolians, Corsicans, and Parisians. She is currently working on a book about her search for the best of all possible worlds.

Sarah McCormic grew up on an island in the Pacific Northwest. She lives in Seattle, where she works as an editor at the University of Washington. Her writing has appeared in the *Seattle Weekly, Bitch* magazine, and *Outside Online.*

Marilyn McFarlane is a freelance writer who has contributed to guidebooks on the West Coast, where she has lived her whole life. She is the author of *Sacred Myths: Stories of World Religions,* an illustrated book of stories from seven spiritual paths. She has four daughters and eleven grandchildren and lives in Portland with her husband and two cats.

Colleen McGuire grew up in rural Indiana farm country and felt compelled to see the world. Before she turned thirty, she had traveled to more than fifty countries. She cycled solo from New York to San Francisco. She lives in Greece and New York and operates a bicycle tour company called CycleGreece.

Liza Monroy has written for *The New York Times; Los Angeles Times; Newsweek; The Village Voice; Time Out New York;* and *Mexico, A Love Story.* She's a book reviewer for *BUST* magazine and a research editor at *JANE,* where she occasionally blogs for its website. She has lived in Mexico, Italy, Greece, the Czech Republic, and the United States.

Pamela S. Stamatiou has been living in Greece since 1990 with her husband and two children. She has a master's degree in international economics and has worked for the Food and Agriculture Organization of the United Nations in Rome, Italy. She is currently enrolled in the UCLA Extension Writers' Program.

Susan Tiberghien, an American living in Switzerland, has published three memoirs—*Looking for Gold, Circling to the Center,* and *Footsteps, A European Album*—as well as shorter work in journals and anthologies. She teaches writing workshops in the United States and in Europe for the International Women's Writing Guild, C. G. Jung Centers, and the Geneva Writers' Group, where she directs the biennial Geneva Writers' Conference.

Davi Walders's poetry and prose have appeared in more than 200 anthologies and journals including *The American Scholar, JAMA, Potomac Review, Crab Orchard Review, Ms.,* and *Washington Woman.* Her poetry collection, *Gifts,* was commissioned by the Milton Murray Foundation for Philanthropy and presented to the Andrew Carnegie Medal of Philanthropy recipients. She developed and directs the Vital Signs Writing Project at National Institutes of Health in Bethesda, Maryland. Her work has been choreographed and performed in New York City and elsewhere and read by Garrison Keillor on National Public Radio's "The Writer's Almanac."

Ronna N. Welsh has cooked professionally for more than ten years as both executive and pastry chef in a number of New York City restaurants, at pastry shops, on farms, and in homes in France, Spain, Greece, and Sicily. She has written articles and developed recipes for the Food Network, *Saveur, Time Out New York, Martha Stewart Living,* and other media. Her culinary work has been featured in *Diario de Alto Aragon,* a Spanish regional newspaper. Welsh is an advocate for sustainable farming and cooking causes and is active in numerous organizations, including the Chefs Collaborative, Women Chefs & Restaurateurs, Slow Food, and the Philosophy of Food Convivium. She is currently writing a book about her travels cooking abroad.

Sara Woster was born and raised in South Dakota. She studied Byzantine iconography in Greece and taught art to kids in France. While living in New York, she began showing her paintings and animation throughout the world, including exhibits in Amsterdam, London, and Japan. She has published several short stories and was recently included in the anthology *The May Queen*. She is finishing up her novel, *Survival Skills*, which has been optioned for a movie. Her next project, *Babe in the Woods*, is a humorous nonfiction account of her summer spent living in a cabin with an outhouse in the woods of Northern Minnesota as she prepares to have a baby under less than modern conditions. When not spending their summers in the woods, Woster and her husband, sculptor Rob Fischer, spend most of the year in Brooklyn, where they revel in their indoor plumbing and eating food not covered in mayonnaise.

About the Editor

Camille Cusumano is the editor of *Mexico, A Love Story; France, A Love Story;* and *Italy, A Love Story,* all published by Seal Press. She is the author of many food and travel articles, several food books, and *The Last Cannoli,* a novel. She lives in San Francisco.